I0084770

Fire Dynamics for Firefighters – edition 2

Compartment Firefighting Series Volume 1

Benjamin Walker BA(Hons) FIFireE (Godiva Award) MSoA EMT

Shan Raffel AFSM EngTech CFIFireE CF

ISBN: 978-0-6451420-0-6

About the authors

Benjamin Walker is a globally acclaimed presenter and international compartment firefighting instructor.

He started his career in the Metropolitan Tyne & Wear Fire Brigade, working and commanding some of Europe's busiest fire stations. Following a spell at a small rural fire department, he took a study sabbatical in the United States, obtaining several fire service certifications and studying FEMA's Emergency Management qualifications.

Returning to the UK to train the London Fire Brigade in compartment firefighting, he was recognised by the Institution of Fire Engineers, winning the Godiva Award and subsequent works and contributions led to award of the Fellowship of the Institution aged 40. He has had operational spells at Fire EMS departments in the USA including riding out with Chicago Fire Department, Newport FD and studying Emergency Medicine at Roger Williams University, Providence, Rhode Island.

In demand as a presenter and instructor, he has taught on multiple occasions at the world's largest conference, FDIC in Indianapolis, and remains determined in his pursuit of reducing firefighter line of duty deaths worldwide. He appears as a firefighting subject expert for Sky News, BBC, Russia Today and many other media outlets, writing for The Guardian, FIRE, Fire Risk Management, Fire Engineering and more.

Ben is the Chief and Director of Ignis Global Ltd, a bespoke Fire and Safety Consultancy in the UK, providing training and safety/risk management advice to Fire Services, industry, and private clients. Ignis Global is also an official education provider of ABBE (Awarding Body for the Built Environment) on behalf of Birmingham City University, courses offered include Diploma and Certificate in Fire Risk Assessment, Award in Fire Door Surveying. Fire Safety Auditors (with WFST), Technical Rescue Instructor (with IRRTC) with many more are also available.

Shan Raffel has served as a career firefighter in Brisbane Australia since 1983. His career took a serious change in 1994 after two of his colleagues were killed in the line of duty while conducting fighting operations in a relatively routine fire in a small motorcycle dealership. The Coroner's report was unable to identify the cause of two extreme fire events that cause severe burns, dislocating them from the hose line and rendering them unconscious.

In 1996, two other colleagues were seriously injured after being caught in an extreme fire event while conducting search and rescue operations in a smoke-laden section of a Backpackers Hostel in Rockhampton.

These events motivated him to develop an extensive report that led to an international study of compartment fire behaviour training (CFBT) in 1997. He studied at the leading training institutions in Sweden and the UK. Over the next three years, he developed the first nationally recognized CFBT program in Australia. Subsequently, he has assisted numerous fire services around the world in the development of their training facilities, instructors, and teaching materials.

In 2009 he was awarded a "Churchill Fellowship" to research "Planning Preparation and Response to Emergencies in Tunnels". This resulted in an intensive ten-week international research tour. This included leading fire services, training centres and tunnel operators in the USA (FDNY), Canada, Germany, Austria, Sweden, Denmark, Norway, and Switzerland. This knowledge was critical in the development of emergency response plans for the 3 largest road tunnels in Australia.

His international training experience spans 26 countries, and his International Compartment Fire Behaviour Instructors program gained international credentialing through the Institution of Fire Engineers recognition process in 2018.
www.linkedin.com/in/shanraffel

Ben and Shan remain at the cutting edge of international operations knowledge and scientific advances. They strive to presenting this essential information in an accessible and clear manner for firefighters wherever they are the world. Stay honest, open, and forthright, without fear.

Foreword

Dan Stephens

Chief Fire and Rescue Advisor and Inspector at Welsh Government

I am very grateful to Ben and Shan for the opportunity to write the foreword for Edition 2 of Fire Dynamics for Firefighters. It is something I very much wanted to do with Edition 1, but circumstances conspired against me preventing me from doing so at the time.

Fire Dynamics for Firefighters is a book written for Firefighters by Firefighters. It presents scientific and technical material in a simple and easily digestible format. I would very much have valued having it available to me as a recruit Firefighter and through the formative stages of my career, in particular when studying for exams.

Irrespective of the point you are at in your career it is a must have for any Firefighter. It provides highly effective underpinning knowledge to compliment National Operational Guidance and will undoubtedly improve the situational awareness and therefore the safety of any Firefighter who reads it. As a serving Chief Fire Officer Edition 1 was a publication I strongly recommended colleagues to read and I maintain that view to this day with Edition 2 which has been enhanced further still by Ben and Shan.

As someone who has the same passion and enthusiasm for my profession today as I did as a recruit I can't praise Ben and Shan highly enough for the contribution they have made to Firefighter safety through Fire Dynamics for Firefighters and the related publications in the series. I am sure you will derive the same value from their great work as I know I have.

Authors' foreword

This book was initially written with the express purpose of making fire dynamics science accessible to Firefighters and practitioners at all levels. Although fire dynamics is a scientific discipline, we kept jargon and mathematics to a minimum wherever possible, with the express intention of this being a basic introduction to fire dynamics.

The success of the book pleasantly surprised, and has been cited in academic papers, used as mandatory reading by the Institution of Fire Engineers' and used by many fire departments, training providers and organisations throughout the world.

As we approached the five year anniversary, having delivered training and assistance to Firefighters all over the world, with the assistance of our friends at IFRA and other charitable organisations, alongside our day jobs as professional Firefighting Instructors, we reflected and bought the books forward to become even more helpful.

Shan developed the IFE's International Tactical Firefighting (Compartment Behaviour Instructors' Programme), of which some of this book addresses parts of the learning outcomes required for successful completion- so we have listed them at the end of each chapter. More are linked in the sequels to this book and of course during the course.

We also realized that during our travels, some Firefighters only have access to a cell phone as a source of information, the developing world often can't afford books- so this edition will also have an "e-copy" or "kindle"- within this we've also added hyper-links to public domain videos, kindly provided often by our friends, which are available on our YouTube channel which is all free. A big thank you to our friends globally for their support with that and we feel it helps to embed the simple learning in this edition.

Hopefully those introduced will want to learn more and progress onto the more technical and detailed publications on this subject.

Think of this book as the first 'stepping stone' onto more detailed and academic publications on this subject.

A sound understanding of the fundamentals of fire development forms the essential foundation of safe and efficient fire and rescue operations. This empowers us to protect our colleagues and the communities we serve.

This book would not have been possible without the innovators in this field who have successfully linked theoretical fire dynamics with the practice of successful and professional firefighting in the field and giving us their time and indulgence with this project. Thank you especially to Bill Gough, Martin Arrowsmith, "The Exbendables", Andrew Starnes, Bobby Halton, David Kay, Matthew Swan, David Payton, Nick Lacey, Sean McKee, Chris Gannon, Steven Burns and anyone else we've overlooked and apologise for.

Dedication

For those that have made the ultimate sacrifice, this has been written to honour your memory, so that others may learn.

Chris Warburton QFES (Brisbane MFB) 1989

Herbert Fennel and Noel Watson QFES 1994

Jeffery Penfold QFES 2001

Paul Barrow Tyne & Wear Metropolitan Fire Brigade 2010

Billy Vinton Tyne & Wear Metropolitan Fire Brigade 2007

Roy Lewis Tyne & Wear Metropolitan Fire Brigade 2012

Never Forgotten.

"If you stand up and be counted, from time to time you may get yourself knocked down. But remember this: A man flattened by an opponent can get up again. A man flattened by **conformity** *stays down for good."*

Thomas J. Watson, Jr

Chapter 1: Basic fire dynamics science for Firefighters

Yes, I know this is the point at which most Firefighters quietly put their feet up, go very quiet, and, to quote the words of Nick Brunacini, 'stare at the sun'…

So, let's be brief, simple and to the point. If you fall asleep during this then I'll personally refund your hard-earned investment in this book. It's based on science but it's not a science textbook, more of a Firefighter's manual. Anything that can be simplified has been. You don't need to be a professor to get your head around this stuff!

Starting simply!

States of matter:

Materials exist in 3 forms: solid, liquid and gas. In a firefighting context we can encounter fuels in these various. Understanding how variations in temperature can affect fuel vapour formation is a critical concept.

Solids:

Solids have defined shapes and the molecules contained within are rigid, structured and ordered like grids or matrixes. Think soldiers on parade and in formation.

Increase the temperature and the molecules lose this rigid structure and begin to move around freely – they become liquids.

Liquids:

Liquids still have a shape but that's only dictated by the container that holds them. Think soldiers on a perfectly square drill ground but moving around with no pattern or order. They're contained but moving freely. For the purposes of fire behaviour, think that the container dictating the shape is the compartment the fire is in.

Increase the temperature again and we have...

Gases:

Gases have absolutely no order or discipline, molecules moving randomly and not contained by any rules, they expand to fill all the available space. These are the 'hippies' of the molecular science world, free spirits.

Some solids bypass the liquid stage and turn directly into gas. These are known as 'subliminates' and the process is known as 'sublimination'.

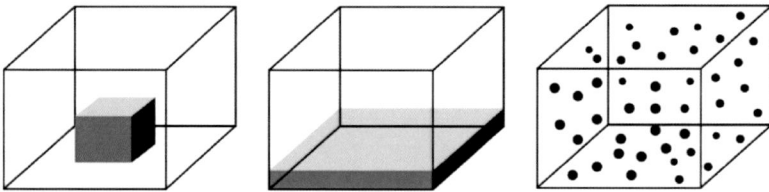

Terms of movement between the states of matter and the point at which sufficient heat is generated to change the matter are defined as followings:

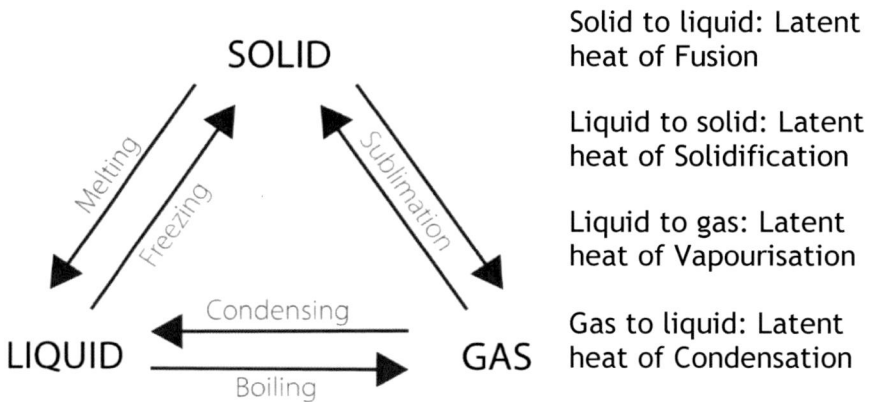

Solid to liquid: Latent heat of Fusion

Liquid to solid: Latent heat of Solidification

Liquid to gas: Latent heat of Vapourisation

Gas to liquid: Latent heat of Condensation

> **For firefighters, how does the volume or shape of a material affect burning?**
>
> A fuel will burn quicker or slower depending on its surface area to volume ratio. Put simply, a single sheet of paper burns faster than a bound 'ream' of hundreds of sheets due to its surface to volume ratio being higher.
>
> In the same way, spilled gasoline (or petrol) on the sidewalk or pavement will vaporise and burn more easily than the same quantity in a container.

Gas laws made simple

'PVT' principles

Gases, as we mentioned, are undisciplined, expanding to take up all available space, (I'm sure 'creative' instructors can add their own metaphors here) but we can alter the volume of the gas by altering the volume of its container.
If we reduce the volume of the container of the gas, the pressure of the gas is increased. The gas molecules occupy a smaller area and collide more frequently, causing pressure.

Volume and pressure are related!

Heating the container causes an increase in this kinetic (movement) energy of the gas molecules causing more collisions and more pressure.

Temperature and pressure are related!
All gases expand by the same amount for the same temperature rise. So, if temperature is related to volume and pressure, and pressure to volume, all of these three concepts are interlinked. **Remember: PVT - it comes up again and again.**

> P – Pressure
> V - Volume
> T – Temperature

The relationships are simply explained by these three simple rules of physics:

Boyle's Law

If the temperature of a gas remains constant, volume is inversely proportional to pressure.
If the pressure applied to a gas doubles - the volume is halved.
If the pressure applied to a gas trebles - the volume become $\frac{1}{3}$
Likewise, if the pressure halves – the volume doubles.

Charles' Law

If the pressure remains constant, gases expand by $\frac{1}{273}$ their volume at $0°c$ for each $1°c$ rise in temperature. A $273°c$ increase in temperature has increased the volume of that gas by 100%
Let us remember as gas volume increases, density decreases, and buoyancy increases- so hotter gases tend to rise- hence why smoke and fire gas rises

Law of Pressures

If a volume of gas is kept constant (such as gas in a container), its pressure is directly proportional to its absolute temperature.
Double the temperature – double the pressure"

For firefighters, how does this affect us?

We all deal with smoke, a buoyant, toxic and flammable mixture of gases and particulates. We often encounter extreme temperatures in the fire compartment and adjacent spaces.

By reducing the temperature of the gas, we reduce the volume of the gas. By cooling the smoke gases, we not only reduce the temperature in the room, but there is also a significant reduction in the volume of these gases. Later in this book we will discuss flammability range and how it is affected by temperature!

By reducing the temperature of the container, we reduce pressure in a closed vessel.

By increasing the volume of the container we reduce the pressure of the gas (ventilation). Ventilation operations can be effective strategies for well-trained crews; however they require excellent communications as part of good overall tactics.

These concepts are very important when we talk about rapid fire developments and tactical approaches later, so remember **PVT- Pressure, Volume, Temperature.**

When a gas is heated it becomes more buoyant and will rise. As the temperature of the gas increases, so does its volume, unless….. it is confined inside a vessel which will result in a temperature increase.

Gas flows

Gas always flows from areas of higher pressure to lower pressure; think of undoing a balloon knot, the gas inside the balloon (which is at a higher pressure) soon escapes to atmosphere at a lower pressure. This is a vital consideration when opening doors to pressurised compartments!
Gases flow in two distinct ways: laminar (smooth flows) and turbulent (excitable) flows. This is important in fire and flame development which we will cover later but keep this in your mind for now!

For firefighters, how do gas flows affect us?

Most compartments contain obstacles and rough surfaces (furniture and fittings) resulting in more turbulent gas flows. Turbulent gas flows result in larger **surface areas** of fire gases (fuel), which increases the reaction rate and flame speeds. In short, it causes fire to spread more rapidly.

Let's remember that our actions can create or affect these gas flows through simple actions such as opening doors, windows or ventilating. Because gas will move from higher to lower pressure areas like the balloon example.

Our tactics in controlling these gas flows are called 'flowpath management'.

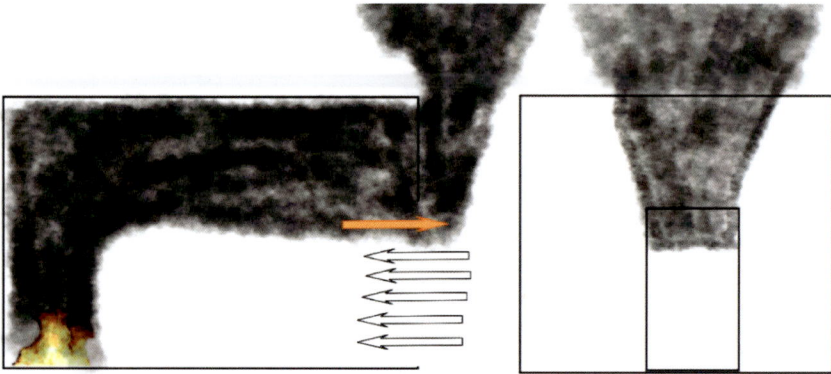

Typical Bi-directional air track. (Raffel)

Here, we can see heated, pressurised fire gases exiting towards an area of low pressure, while cool air enters through the same opening. This is known as a 'bi-directional flow path'.

Some firefighters term the cold air flowing towards and feeding a fire the 'airtrack' while the exiting hot gases the 'flowpath'.
For the purposes of standardisation, we shall refer to both of these as flowpaths. Cold air moving 'towards' the fire, we'll call the 'inlet flowpath', while exiting hot gases moving towards the exit, we'll call the 'outlet flowpath'.

If we look at the next figure, we can see that hot air is exiting through one opening (exhaust vent) while cooler air enters through another (inlet vent). This completes a flowpath from inlet to outlet that is known as 'uni-directional flowpath' (the gas flows one way).

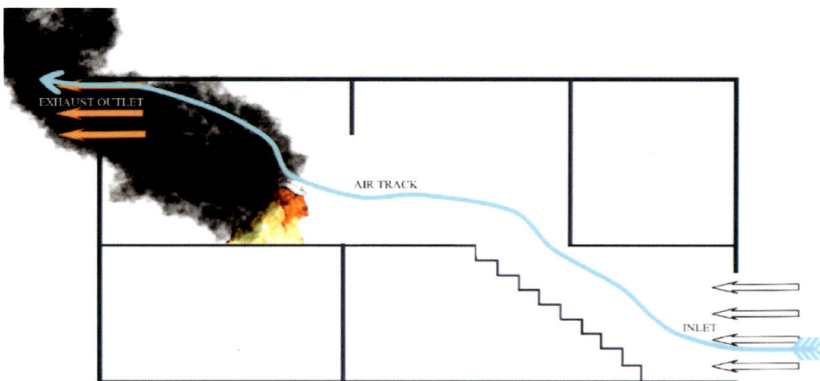

Uni-directional Flowpath (Raffel)

For firefighters, what do flowpaths mean for me?

It is of the utmost importance to understand the effect of opening and closing doors and windows, creating these flowpaths and influencing fire development by either restricting or providing oxygen (via the inlet flowpath) to the fire.

Gaseous fuels can move rapidly and turbulently, and fire can develop swiftly with tragic consequences. We must be both cautious of letting air in and letting fire gases out, the route taken by those fire gases and our physical position on or off that route.

If we are located on the 'inlet flowpath' side of a fire that's got a unidirectional flowpath and the hot gases are exiting away from us, we can attack and make progress quickly.

If we are on a bi-directional flowpath (both inlet and outlet route – see **Figure 1**) we have to address the exiting gases as a priority, by use of water, assess and control them before moving forward into position. This movement pattern is covered in detail in our book "Fighting Fire".

If we are situated on the ***outlet flowpath side of a uni-directional flowpath*** we are in ***an extremely dangerous place*** that has potential for us to become caught in a 'tube/funnel' of fire.

There is also potential for a blow-torch effect should the inlet point become 'wind driven' or further opened to admit more air. **This is not the place to be!**

In discussions with eminent Fire Service leaders including Chief Bobby Halton (Albuquerque, New Mexico, USA) we have applied a term from the US military to describe this area: 'the kill zone', or the 'fatal funnel'.

In depth coverage of positioning and tactics are covered in our book "Fighting Fire".

Do not get caught in the KILL ZONE and become a statistic!

Chapter 1: revision questions

List the three states of matter.

- What is the name of the point at which a solid will turn into a liquid?
- What are substances called that turn directly from solids into gases?
- What happens to the pressure of a gas if the volume of the container reduces?
- What is the name of the gas law that governs that rule of physics?
- List two effects of a volume of gas rising. In a fixed size container if the temperature of a gas trebles.
- What happens to the pressure? List the two types of gas flows.
- Use a balloon example to describe movement of gas.
- What can Firefighters do to control gas flows and what is this known as?
- Name two types of flowpath and briefly explain each.
- What is the term that can be used to describe any position on the outlet flowpath (between the fire and its exhaust vent point) which emphasises the danger of positioning in this area?

This chapter covers the following learning outcomes form the Aus-Rescue International Compartment Fire Behaviour Instructor Level 1, IFE recognised training course:

Learning Outcome	Description
1.	Understand the fundamental principles of combustion reactions and the factors influence the speed of reaction
1.1	Describe and explain the fire triangle and the role of chain carriers
1.2	Explain the ignition process in solids, liquids and gases

The following videos assist with understanding of this chapter- find them at the YouTube channel: Ben Walker & Shan Raffel Firefighter Training tinyurl.com/2xaeb4yu

Video and Hyperlinks:
3 States of Matter - tinyurl.com/2kmhaujs
What is Matter? - tinyurl.com/bv5d6ady
Vapourisation and Condensation - https://tinyurl.com/y279jjkn
What is Air Pressure- Balloons - https://tinyurl.com/7xmsen4w
Laminar Flow vs Turbulent Flow - https://tinyurl.com/rvfknmk4
Bi-Directional Flowpath - https://tinyurl.com/s82y8uu2

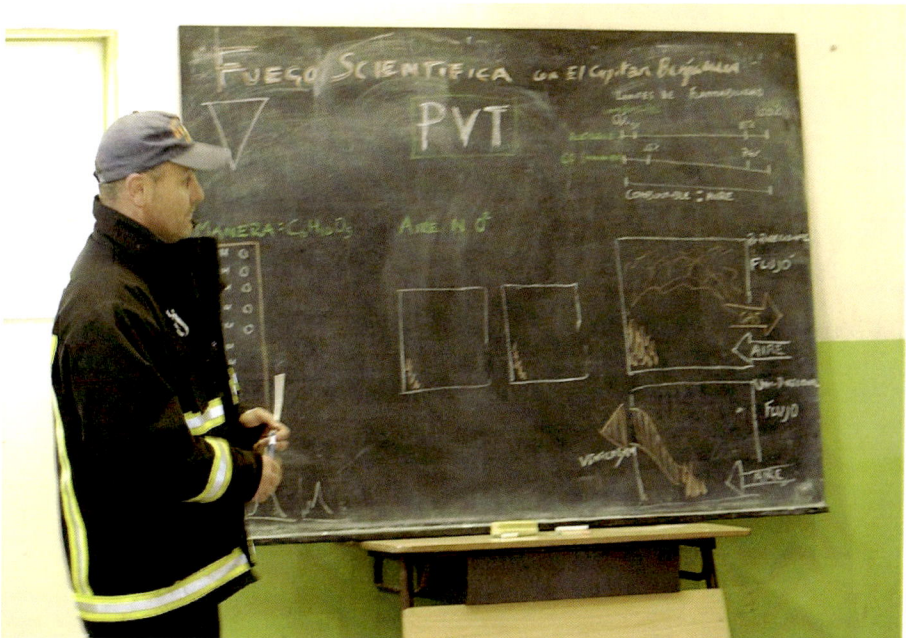

Teaching PVT in Castellano (South American Spanish) presents its own challenges, but the principles remain the same (photograph - Walker IFRA 2015)

Chapter 2: The combustion process

What is combustion?

The combustion process can best be described by breaking it down into the components of itself:

- *First, what is it? It is a chemical reaction, which is irreversible.*

- *Second, what's involved? Fuel, heat and oxygen.*

- *Third, what are the results of this chemical reaction? Energy is produced in the form of heat and light.*

Therefore, perhaps a comprehensive definition of combustion could be:

'An irreversible chemical reaction between fuel and an oxidiser that produces energy in the form of heat and light.'

Complete Combustion is where all available fuel is used due to an unlimited source of ventilation or oxygen. Incomplete Combustion occurs when all available fuel cannot be burned due to insufficient oxygen. This is the environment that Firefighters encounter most often.

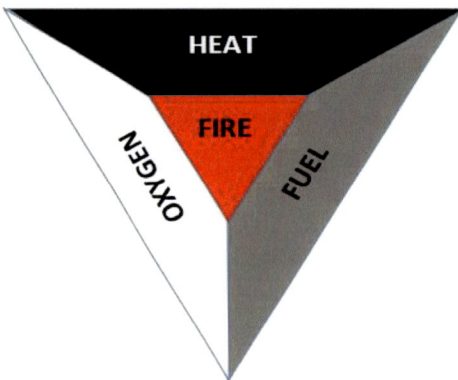

The basic fire triangle that all boy scouts learn is shown in Figure 3 in a slightly different way.

Note that the graphic is shown with the point at the bottom. We will cover this slightly later in the book.

A traditional approach is that if you remove one of the elements of the triangle then the combustion process will cease. While that may be the foundation upon which we base our tactics, indeed, water cools and removes heat, there are exceptions to the rule and due to modern lifestyles, these are becoming far more frequent.

Oxygen

A likely scenario can be encountered where fuel and heat exist in sufficient quantities to support combustion, all that is required is for oxygen to be added to complete the chemical reaction and initiate flaming combustion. The addition of oxygen can be caused by as simple an action as opening a door allowing air (containing oxygen) to flow towards the heat and fuel source. In the efforts to locate and extinguish a fire, the firefighter must remain alert to this possibility and consider the effects of opening and closing doors en-route to the fire. This is called 'flow path management'.

- If a fire has insufficient oxygen to support combustion it, its growth and movement are dictated by the amount of ventilation available and is known as 'ventilation controlled'.

- If a fire has sufficient ventilation to continue to burn until all available fuel is used, it is dictated by that fuel and known as 'fuel controlled'.

A ventilation-controlled fire can affect the other two elements of the fire triangle. If combustion ceases due to a lack of available oxygen, then temperatures may reduce and heat energy also. However, fuel can still be available, and heat may remain sufficient to auto ignite this fuel once oxygen is introduced and the fuel mixes to within its 'limits of flammability'. This phenomenon is covered later in this chapter.

While oxygen is a requirement for combustion, it's important to remember that there are fuels that produce or release oxygen when subjected to heat and the pyrolysis process. These are known as oxidizing agents. Peroxides are a common example of this.

Fuel

Fuel can be referred to as the 'fuel package' and can be found in any of the three states of matter: solid, liquid or gas. When exposed to heat a fuel goes through a process of chemical decomposition known as 'pyrolysis'. In short, the heat causes the fuel to move through its matter states while breaking down into its component chemicals in vapour form.

These chemical components are released as gases, known as pyrolysates and volatiles and may bond with other components contained within that fuel to form a number of gases. This is also sometimes referred to as 'off-gassing'. These gases are what we have referred to for years as smoke. Let's now re-name them 'fire gases', a.k.a. unburned pyrolysates/volatiles/pyrolysis products.

These fire gases can be full of energy, which, if a fire is burning freely will be released and contribute to the fire as a fuel. But the presence of heat without flame, known as "smouldering ", can cause pyrolysis and the release of fire gases that are full of energy, but unable to be burned off and contribute to the fire (yet!). This is an extremely dangerous situation, that we will cover in the Rapid Fire Development chapters on Backdraft and Fire Gas Ignition.

Sometimes fuel doesn't pass through a liquid stage to release gases, these types of fuel are known as 'subliminals' and this process is called 'sublimination'.

For example, the chemical equation for wood is $C^6 H^{10} O^5$. This can be broken down as follows to represent the atoms contained within:

CCCCCC HHHHHHHHHH OOOOO

When heat exposure causes pyrolysis, the $C^6 H^{10} O^5$ releases these atoms which can bond with others released to form the following:

If 2x Hydrogen atoms bond with 1x Oxygen atom it creates H^2O or water vapour.

If 1x Carbon Atom bonds with 2x Oxygen atom it creates CO^2 or carbon dioxide.

If 1x Carbon Atom bonds with 1 x Oxygen atom it creates CO or carbon monoxide.

If Carbon atoms don't bond but are released, they form the substance we commonly known as 'soot' or unburned carbon molecules.

These atoms are all present in wood, or $C^6H^{10}O^5$, but if we are also burning in normal atmosphere, we must also consider the presence of the chemical elements that compose the air we breathe.

Air is 99% composed of Nitrogen (N) and Oxygen (O). It also contains very small quantities of the noble gases, which can have an effect on fire development at an extremely scientific level.

Thus, when we consider the Carbon, Hydrogen and Oxygen already existing in the wood and add Nitrogen, we can form dangerous mixtures such as HCN known as Hydrogen Cyanide.

Although in small percentages, air also contain these noble gases:

Name of Gas:	Symbol	% in Air
Argon	Ar	0.9 %
Carbon dioxide	CO_2	0.03 %
Neon	Ne	0.002 %
Helium	He	0.0005 %
Methane	CH_4	0.0002 %
Krypton	Kr	0.0001 %
Hydrogen	H_2	0.00005 %
Xenon	Xe	0.000009 %

If we apply the same process of pyrolysis to all of these elements and mixtures, we can see that there is potential for creating a large number of different gases, with a variety of features such as toxicity and flammability.

And this is only by burning a piece of wood in air. Let's consider that modern dwellings and workplaces contain furniture, fixtures and contents that are made up of far more complex chemical elements than a wooden bench.

There is clearly potential for firefighters to be operating in an environment composed of a number of chemicals in gaseous form, as smoke, before the fire is even located.

For firefighters, how does smoke (gaseous fuels) affect our approach?

If we consider that the majority of these gases are flammable, then we must consider that all smoke is unburned fuel, toxic, flammable and ignitable. A firefighter would not walk through a pool of gasoline and without recognising it as fuel, so why do we continue to walk through unburned fuel in the form of smoke when carrying out our operations at fires?

This environment was termed in 2005 as the '3D environment'. The presence of fire gases is three dimensional (3D) and requires a 3D or 'all around' approach to successfully address this and reduce risks.

3D Firefighting 2005, Paul Grimwood, Ed Hartin, John McDonough & Shan Raffel

Flammability Limits

A relationship between Fuel and Air

Flammability limits are the ratios of concentration between a fuel in vapour (gaseous) form and the air in the immediate surrounding atmosphere.

Flammability limits are widely categorised into the following:

- Lower Explosive Limit

- Upper Explosive Limit

- Ideal Mixture (aka Stochiometric Mixture).

Lower Explosive Limit

This is the lowest concentration of fuel to air that will sustain combustion. It is sometimes referred to as a **'lean mixture'**. If the concentration dips below this it can be referred to as **'too lean to burn'**.

Upper Explosive Limit

This is the highest concentration of fuel to air that will sustain combustion. It is sometimes referred to as a 'rich mixture'. If the ratio of fuel to air is too high it can be known as 'too rich to burn'. This can be an extremely dangerous situation and if a fire has been or is present it can be referred to as 'ventilation controlled' – it's just waiting for introduction of air to 'dilute' it back down to within its flammable limits where it can burn freely.

Ideal Mixture/Stochiometric Mixture

This is the ratio of fuel to air where a substance can burn most efficiently and with the greatest force.

What can affect the flammable range? (PVT)

For many flammable mixtures, the flammability range is widened when the temperature is increased

Decreasing pressure narrows the flammability range by increasing the lower flammability limit and decreasing the upper flammability limit. (Burgess and Wheeler 1911).

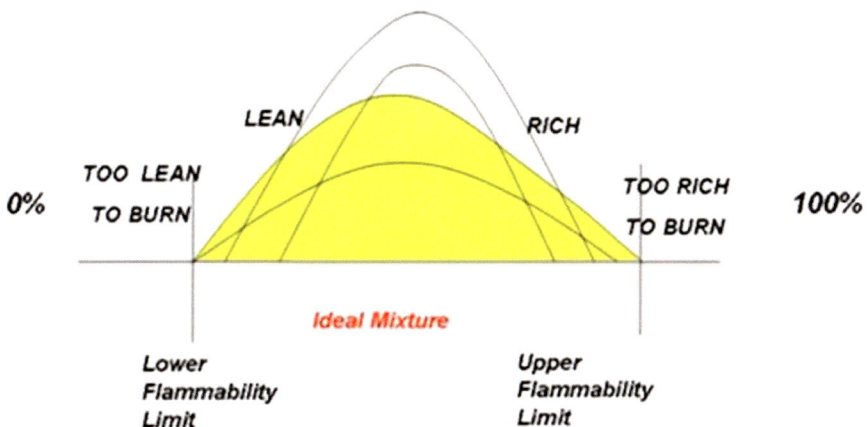

Examples of flammability limits. Credits to Merseyside Fire and Rescue. UK

For firefighters, what do the flammability limits mean for us?
As we can see, all fuels need a supply of oxygen to burn. We can take steps to control the amount of air a fuel can mix with through 'flowpath management' and either ventilating (opening) or shutting down (anti-ventilating) compartments. We must be aware that we may be proceeding into danger if we know that a fuel/air mix is above its Upper Explosive Limit and 'too rich'. In that case, if we open doors, we may allow airflow to dilute it down into its flammability limits. It shows that fuels are in vapour form everywhere in the 3D environment and must be dealt with to reduce our exposure to risk.

We have shown that products of combustion such as carbon monoxide have wide flammable ranges and can burn across a wide ratio of concentration with air. Modern compartments have more materials than wood releasing $C^6H^{10}O^5$ and 'fire gases' are a combination of a number of fuels in vapour form. A vigilant and well-prepared firefighter knows this and regards all vapours in the 3D environment as flammable fuels ready to burn. Smouldering fires may lead to the release of high energy products in those vapours, waiting to be able to contribute when a fire can burn, potentially with deadly consequences.

Vapours, and unburned pyrolysis products are flammable! Note the exiting gases auto-ignited when the door was opened. (Photograph, Raffel CFBT-Thailand)

Passive agents

Passive agents are materials within any compartment that absorb energy in the form of heat. All elements within a compartment's structure or furnishing act as passives for a short time, until temperature increases, pyrolysis begins, and the thermal capacity of that material is reached.

At this point the material is no longer passive and actively contributes to the fire as fuel in the form of pyrolysis products or by transferring heat back into the compartment or conducting it to other areas and contributing to fire spread.

Gases released by passives undergoing pyrolysis can also act as passive agents, water vapour and carbon dioxide given off in this way can suppress fire development in early stages and localised areas.

So what do passives do?

Passive agents take away energy from the fire which can slow its growth progress for such a time until they can absorb no more energy and start actively contributing to the fire's growth as fuel.

Heat

Heat is perhaps the most misunderstood of the traditional three elements of the fire triangle. To dispel a popular misconception, we need to know the difference between temperature and heat.

Heat is a measure of the energy contained by a body, both its potential (stored) and kinetic (moving) energy. It is measured in joules (J).

Temperature is a measure of the kinetic (moving) energy of that body. As heat is introduced, the molecules move faster and collide more frequently, producing more heat. Temperature is a measure of these collisions.

However, these are not inextricably linked. For example, the heat created by raising 500 litres of water to 100°C substantially greater than that created by raising one litre to 100°C although the temperature is the same.

Or, to use another example, a cup of tea at 80°C is a higher temperature than a swimming pool at 30°C, but because the swimming pool is clearly a much larger quantity of water, the total thermal energy it contains (its heat) is a great deal higher.

The formula to measure heat is as follows

$$Q = CMT$$

Where Q is heat energy, C is specific heat capacity, M is mass of the body and T is its temperature.

Auto ignition temperatures

When a fuel reaches a certain temperature, there is enough kinetic energy in it to ignite it without the presence of a flame or the introduction of an external ignition source.

Substance	AIT °C
Triethylborane	–20 °C
Silane	21 °C
White phosphorus	34 °C
Carbon disulfide	90 °C
Diethyl ether	160 °C
Gasoline (Petrol)	247–280 °C
Ethanol	363 °C
Diesel or Jet A-1	210 °C
Butane	405 °C
Paper	218–246 °C
Leather/Parchment	200–212 °C
Magnesium	473 °C
Hydrogen	536 °C

Flashpoints and firepoints

When a liquid substance reaches a certain temperature there can be fire gases (pyrolysates/volatiziles/vapours) released that form an ignitable mixture in air that, when an ignition source is introduced, causes combustion to occur.

If the substance does not continue to burn when the gnition ource is removed this is known as the **'flash point'**.

If the substance continues to burn once the ignition source is removed then this is known as the **'fire point'.**

Accepted definitions are:
Flash Point: the lowest temperature at which a substance vapourises so that the introduction of an ignition source causes a flame to momentarily 'flash' across the surface of the fuel.

Fire Point: the lowest temperature at which a substance vapourises so that the introduction of an ignition source results in continued combustion once the ignition source is removed.

For firefighters, how does heat affect our approach?

We now know that heat causes the production of more fuel in gaseous form from pyrolysis, (potentially containing significant energy, and unless we intervene, these vapours can auto ignite. If these vapours have collected elsewhere we potentially have a room full of fuel and oxygen ready to combust ferociously that we don't expect. We need to reduce temperatures and heat.

Heat release rate

Heat release rate (or HRR) is a measure of power or the heat energy that is released per measure of time by a fire. It is influenced by many factors including the shape of a fuel and its surface area, for example, a sheet of paper burns more quickly and releases its heat energy more quickly than a log – although the log can generate more heat and greater temperatures over a longer period it releases it more slowly over a greater period of time.

It should be noted that the heat release rate of a fire dictates its size and its speed of growth. If the HRR is higher, then the pyrolysis process is quicker, more gaseous fuel is released and more oxygen is used up, resulting in incomplete combustion and quantities of unburned fuel in a ventilation controlled environment. This is the MOST IMPORTANT factor in the intensity, speed and development of fire.

Bens' old colleague and adventurer, Station Officer Jim Dave of the States of Jersey Fire & Rescue Service (retired), emphasises the importance of heat release rate in this extract from his Masters' Degree dissertation:

"Heat Release Rates The single most important variable in fire

Heat release rate (HRR) is the amount of energy that is released when a substance burns. The extent to which this consequence occurs is dependent on the material and ventilation parameters that are present at the time of combustion. It is often over looked and seen as just another measurement of data that has little significance. It is, in fact, the most single important variable in the development of fire.

"Heat release rate is the driving force that influences pretty much all other variables of the fire environment". *As HRR increases, temperature and the rate of temperature change both increase, accelerating fire development. In addition, increased HRR results in reduced oxygen concentration and increased production of gaseous and particulate products of incomplete combustion.*

For firefighters, it is important that HRR directly relates to flow rate required for fire control and for tactical decision making if the HRR is known or can be predicted due to dwelling type. Heat release rate will also influence the engineer when using design fires for prediction.

Accurate heat release rate measurements provide essential information in defining the fire safety characteristics of products. The fuels of primary interest are those found in domestic type properties and include wood, plastics, foam materials used in furnishings (such as polyurethane), wire insulation (such as polyvinyl chloride), and carpet materials (such as nylon).

Heat release rate is a key predictor of the hazard of a fire, directly related to the rate at which heat and toxic gases build up in a compartment or the rate at which they are driven into more remote spaces. Heat release rates on the order of 1MW to 3MW are typical energies released during the tests. These are fairly common in a room that has flashed over (ventilation permitting) or from a single large object such as a bed or sofa.

Most fire deaths are the result of toxic inhalation due to the products of combustion. There are many variables that control the burning rate but it remains the HRR that has the biggest influence on these fire hazards. The ability to measure HRR in compartment fires is relatively new, to that end in is important to recognise that HRR is the best predictor of fire hazard assessment."

Dave J (2012) *Heat Release Rate: The single most important variable in fire.* From MSc Fire Dynamics dissertation, University of Leeds.

Heat Release Rate versus temperature

Underwriters' Laboratories and the National Institute for Science & Technology (UL/NIST) draw a distinction between HRR and temperature using candles as an example. One candle and ten candles (of the same type, size and composition) burn at the same temperature, but the ten candles release ten times the energy, hence ten times the heat release rate.

The previous graphic below shows a single candle that will burn at a temperature of 500-1400°C and give off a Heat Release Rate (HRR) of 80 watts.

Also shown are ten candles of the same type and size. These also burn at a temperature of 500-1400°C, yet produce a Heat Release Rate of 800 watts!

Methods of heat transfer

Heat can be transferred three ways:

- Conduction
- Convection
- Radiation

Heat transfer can be measured in terms of the heat transferred over a measured area in a measured amount of time. This is known as 'heat flux'.

Let's briefly examine each of these in turn.

Conduction

Conduction is the transfer of heat energy through direct contact of materials. For example, our friends in Eastern Kentucky, Greg Gorbett and Jim Pharr in *Fire Dynamics* (2011) cite the example of a metal rod being held in a flame. The part of the metal rod inside the flame is increasing in temperature, so there is more molecular movement (collisions). These begin to strike and affect the neighbouring molecules.

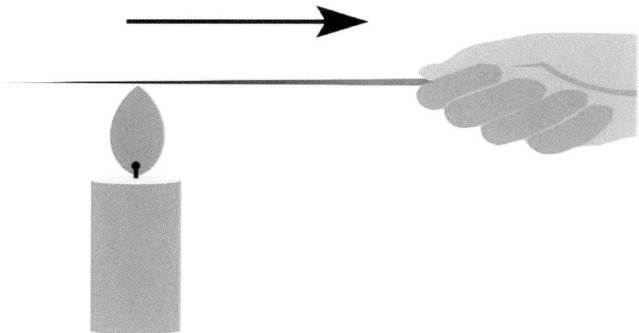

Firefighters should be aware that certain materials conduct heat extremely well and transfer and subsequent ignitions can occur in this way. Other materials do not conduct well and are known as **'insulators'**.

> **For firefighters, how does conduction affect us?**
>
> Heat can be transferred by conduction to other compartments causing fires to spread. Fire departments with ships in port will be acutely aware of metal bulkheads conducting heat to adjacent holds when ships are on fire.

Convection

Convection is the transfer of heat energy through a 'fluid medium'. Beware here that the term 'fluid' does not necessarily mean a liquid. It is far more likely that the fluid medium encountered by firefighters is air.

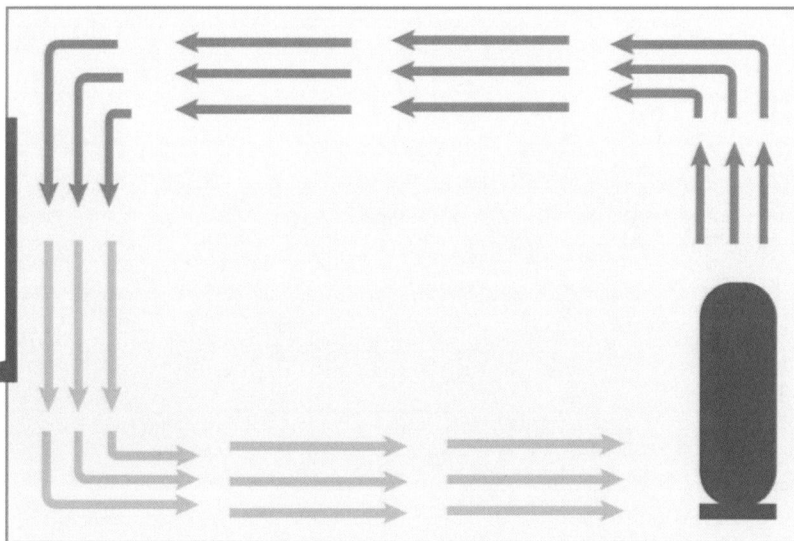

Note the heat rises from the heater while cool air is drawn in towards the heat source at the lower levels as it cools and falls.

In a compartment, heated air/fire gas flows past a solid object and there is a temperature difference. The motion of the fluid and the conduction through air of molecules in the fluid, causes increased molecule activity (collisions) in the solid and therefore a rise in temperature (kinetic heat energy) in the solid.

Convection can transfer heat either 'naturally' or 'forced'; consider how a hot pie cools down when you blow onto the surface (forced). This type of forced heat transfer should also be remembered when managing flowpaths as the actions of the firefighters may change the direction and speed of how the 'fluid medium' flows, affecting heat transfer and fire spread.

For firefighters

How does convection affect me? In addition to managing flow paths, our nozzle techniques can rapidly increase a convection speed and fire spread if we misapply them.

Radiation

Radiation is the transfer of heat energy through electromagnetic waves. This can happen whether a material is in a solid, liquid or gaseous form. Radiation does not require any material such as a conductor or a fluid medium to transfer its energy.

The transfer of heat energy to earth by the sun is an example of radiation.

Radiant heat transfer is generally responsible for fire spread to other materials in a compartment fire. The radiant heat from the flame can ignite other fuels, and the radiant heat from the smoke layer moving downward can increase the spread of fire and progress it towards becoming a fully developed fire – the flashover stage.

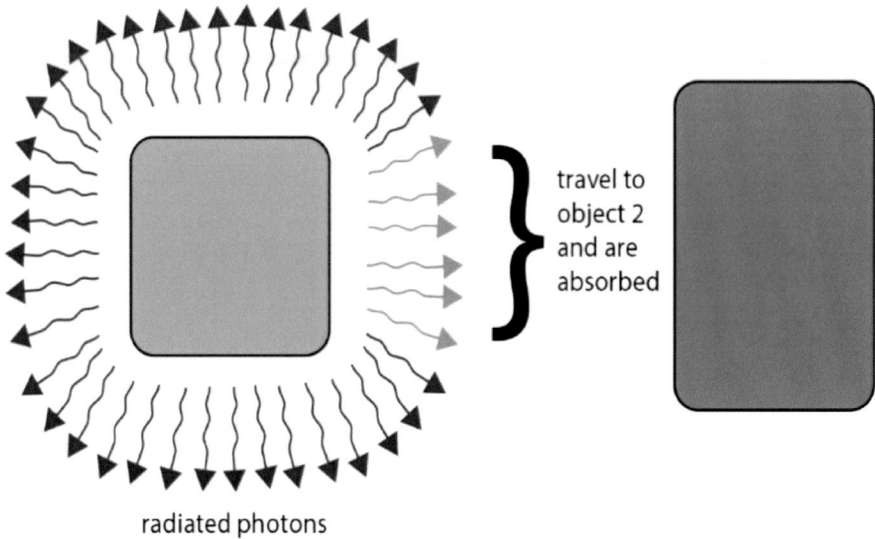

radiated photons

Firefighters should note that the biggest heat transfer process (thus the biggest cause of fire spread) in fire is radiation via soot particles in the smoke/gas. Convection and conduction only form part of heat transfer in lesser ratios than radiation.

Chapter 2: revision questions

- Define combustion.

- Explain the difference between complete and incomplete combustion.

- What are fuels known as that release oxygen when subjected to heat?

- Define pyrolysis.

- Explain the difference between heat and temperature.

- Define the terms 'flash point', 'fire point' and 'auto-ignition temperature'.

- What is Heat Release Rate and give two examples that affect it?

- What is the term that refers to measuring heat transfer in known timescales and over known measured areas?

- List the three types of heat transfers with examples.

- What is the name for materials that do not conduct heat energy well?

- Which of the heat transfer processes is the biggest contributor to fire development?

International Compartment Fire Behaviour Training Instructor Course:

This chapter covers the information needed for the following learning outcomes;

Learning Outcome	Description
1.3	Explain complete combustion, incomplete combustion and passive agents
1.4	Describe flammable limits and the impact of variations in temperature and pressure.
1.5	Explain the chemistry of combustion in solids, liquids, gases, dusts and vapour phases
1.6	Explain how heat energy can be transferred via conduction, convection and radiation
1.7	Explain extinguishing principles in terms of actions that can disrupt the chemical reaction by removing one of more of the sides of the fire triangle
2. Understand how fire develops and spreads within compartments	Understand how fire develops and spreads within compartments

The following videos assist with understanding of this chapter- find them at the YouTube channel: **Ben Walker & Shan Raffel Firefighter Training;** tinyurl.com/2xaeb4yu

Video and Hyperlinks:
Heat Transfer- Conduction https://tinyurl.com/tndd8d5t
Heat Transfer - Convection https://tinyurl.com/36w2fbax
Heat Transfer- Conduction, Convection, Radiation https://tinyurl.com/fvfuxxtw
Heat Release Rate- A visual demonstration https://tinyurl.com/u37k29db
Pyrolysis in Action https://tinyurl.com/4ewd2kav
Smoke (Pyrolysis products is fuel!) https://tinyurl.com/2j39hv4x
Different Materials- Different Pyrolysis https://tinyurl.com/4ewd2kav
Flash Point, Fire Point & Auto-Ignition Temperature https://tinyurl.com/37ce68n7
Flammability Limits and Stoichiometry https://tinyurl.com/dku42fs6
Old School Flammable Range https://tinyurl.com/39jy99bs
Too rich to burn- above UEL- a warning for Firefighters https://tinyurl.com/zvrf3den
Flammable Range- finding out the hard way https://tinyurl.com/475uk2rt

London Fire Brigade Training School/Babcock International.Compartment Fire Behaviour Training Instructors Course.   December 2014

Working with some of the Instructors for the London Fire Brigade. 2014.

LIFE SAVING: Fire officers learn to deal with the deadly smoke from synthetic building materials

Shan Raffel introduces CFBT to Australia in 1997.

Chapter 3: Flames

What is a flame?

Simply answered, a flame is the visible 'combustion zone'
where gases increase in temperature and therefore volume.
Increased volume leads to less density and increased
buoyancy of gases.

There are two distinct types of flame: 'premixed' and 'diffusion'.

*We have established the elements of combustion and covered in
slightly more detail heat, oxygen and fuels. So how does that relate
to us as firefighters?*

*Let's start by revising the types of gas flow then looking at how
flames develop, beginning with the types of flame we encounter.*

Types of Gas Flows

Laminar flows:

Laminar flows have a defined direction and movement – gas
molecules move along pathways liked a bunch of dried spaghetti
strands. Molecules on different strands may move at different
speeds, but all molecules on the same strand move at the same
speed. Strands never cross and molecules never collide.
Laminar flows move smoothly over flat surfaces.

LAMINAR FLOW

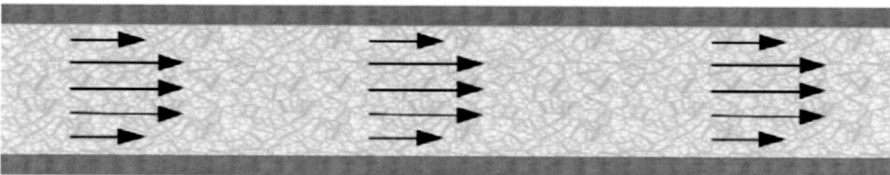

TURBULENT FLOW

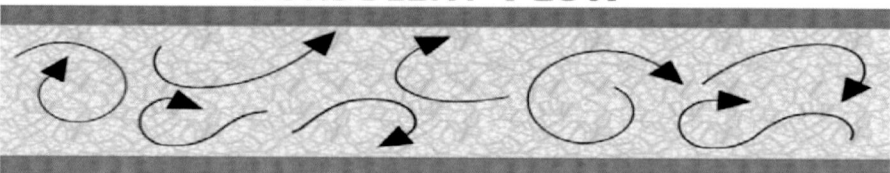

Turbulent flows:

The turbulent gas flow has a definite direction but has random changes of velocity and direction within. It has fast flows over rough surfaces and obstacles.

Premixed flames

Premixed flames are where fuel is well mixed with an oxidant (in the right proportions). For ignition to occur, energy must be supplied by an ignition spark. A self-sustaining flame will then establish around the ignition source and propagate outwards in all directions.

Premixed flames usually have laminar gas flows which are mainly found in industry and are not generally commonly found in firefighting, for example Bunsen Burners.

The flame consists of a zone where cold unburnt gases (reactants) are transferred into hot, burnt gas (products). As the volume of hot gas is increased (remember PVT – increased temperature means increased volume) the flame front is pushed outwards from the ignition point like a balloon skin.

Remember:

- Pre-mixtures have to exist within flammability limits.

- The ideal ratio of fuel to air is the 'stoichiometric mixture' of 'ideal mixture'

- For each mixture there is a 'burning velocity' at which a pre-mixed flame will propagate through a stationary gas.

- If a pre-mixture flows into a flame with a laminar flow with a speed equal to the burning velocity then a flame can be held steady (for example, gas rings on a cooker or, again, a Bunsen burner).

Turbulent gas flows can increase flame speeds faster than burning velocity. These flows cause the flame front to 'wrinkle', increasing its surface area and therefore the reaction rate, increasing the burnt gas produced. Supersonic flame speeds accompanied with a shockwave are known as 'detonation'.

Diffusion flames

There are two types of diffusion flame.

- Laminar diffusion.
- Turbulent diffusion.

Laminar diffusion flames

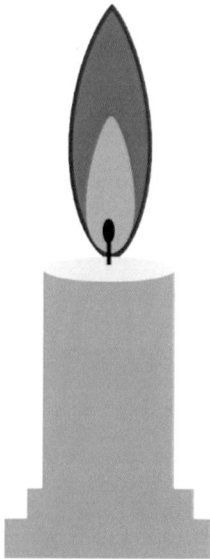

The best-known example of this is a candle.

Fuel vapour rises slowly from the wick in a laminar flow and 'molecular diffusion' dominates.

This means that the molecules move away from the source (the wick), and outwards to areas of lower concentration, like gases moving from high to low pressure areas. Note the alteration of the flammability ratios as the flame climbs and mixes with oxygen, moving towards complete combustion.

Turbulent diffusion flames

Turbulent diffusion flames can be found, for example, in industrial burners where fuel is injected at high velocities (spray-jets), which causes turbulence at the interface and produces a flame with a large surface area.

In this case it is the large interface area (not molecular diffusion) that governs the rate of mixing. Have a look at the example below of a fire-breather spraying fuel into the ignition source and producing a large surface area flame.

Fires that are above one cubic metre in volume produce turbulent diffusion flames. This turbulence is created by the buoyancy of the gas (*remember PVT – increased volume reduces density and increases buoyancy*).

Inside the flames are areas of high temperature and low oxygen. In these areas fuel vapours are subjected to pyrolysis and partial oxidization (mixing with oxygen). This forms and releases products of incomplete combustion (carbon/soot) which as we know can be unburnt fuel in gaseous form (remember the 3D environment!).

For firefighters- what do flames tell us?

It is apparent that the flames we encounter most in compartment fires will be turbulent diffusion flames. We should remember that these generate a quantity of unburned fuel through pyrolysis which increases the danger of our working environment.

Also, we can see that turbulent diffusion flames in a turbulent gas flow (including airflows) can result in fast flame speeds and burning velocities, sometimes even faster than the speed of sound (detonation). This shows that the fire can move very swiftly through unburned fuel, spreading and potentially cutting of our exit routes or causing us harm if we fail to address the 3D environment and make progress to extinguish the fire.

Chapter 3: revision questions

- What is a flame?

- List the two types of flame and two versions of one type giving examples of each.

- What is produced inside flames in areas of high temperature but low oxygen?

- Which two factors need to be the same to hold a flame steady in a cooker's gas ring?

- What are supersonic flame speeds with a shockwave known as?

- Which factor affects the turbulence in fires larger than one cubic metre?

- What should firefighters consider when encountering turbulent diffusion flames in a turbulent gas flow?

- Using PVT principles, briefly describe how they affect flammable range

International Compartment Fire Behaviour Training Instructor Course:

This chapter covers the information needed for the following learning outcomes;

Learning Outcome	Description
1.2	Explain the ignition process in solids, liquids and gases
1.3	Explain complete combustion, incomplete combustion and passive agents
1.4	Describe flammable limits and the impact of variations in temperature and pressure.
1.5	Explain the chemistry of combustion in solids, liquids, gases, dusts and vapour phases
2.2	Explain the factors which affect the development and spread of a compartment fire including geometry, linings, and fuel package location

The following videos assist with understanding of this chapter- find them at the YouTube channel: **Ben Walker & Shan Raffel Firefighter Training;** tinyurl.com/2xaeb4yu

Video and Hyperlinks:
Laminar v Turbulent Diffusion Flame https://tinyurl.com/bp83uawn
Pre-mixed v Diffusion Flame https://tinyurl.com/zu7fmu2s
Zones of Candle Flame https://tinyurl.com/kmd8upza
Defining Burning Velocity https://tinyurl.com/f29npam3
Flame Breathers https://tinyurl.com/2rpurp29

Chapter 4: Fire growth

So how do fires grow? Let's use a single compartment as an example with very basic furnishings, which we shall say are wood based for the purposes of this exercise.

What we know:

- We know that we have fuel in there, we have a reasonably good idea of the chemical composition of that furniture: carbon, hydrogen, and oxygen.

- We know that after pyrolysis these can be mixed with elements of air (and pyrolysis products from other furniture in the compartment) such as nitrogen and oxygen to form numerous flammable and toxic gases, which are all '3D fuels'.

- We know we have air – as a rule, we like to be able to breathe in our rooms.

What we need to find out:

What we don't perhaps know is where that air is coming from or how it is flowing through the room. This is where flowpath management starts to become important.

If we know that we have a window open on the north side of the room with wind coming through from that direction, flowing towards a door on the south side of the room, then we know that there could be a flowing 'fluid medium' transferring heat to solids it passes, causing the fire to spread in that direction.

If we don't know which direction that air is flowing then we have to be careful of creating inlet flowpaths both toward the fire that complete the combustion triangle and allow burning to take place, but also creating outlet flowpaths that allow hot gases to flow away from and spread the fire.

This could potentially place us in danger if we are caught between the fire and the outlet point. (Remember that turbulent flames and gas flows can rapidly increase speed of fire spread!)

So do we have heat? Heat will come from the ignition source originally and will self-sustain once a fuel is heated to its fire point.

The proportion of fuel to heat to air, and the location of the fire in the compartment, are crucial to how a fire develops.

If we look at Shan's graphic below, we can see the bi-directional flowpath.

If a fire develops in the middle of a room, it will draw in air (convection) from a 360° radius.

Therefore, the plume of *the flame will not rise as high into the air attempting to get air to create a diffused flame.*

If a fire is against a wall, however, it can only draw air from 180°, and *so will reach higher towards ceilings to attempt to get air and burn.*

Put the flame into the corner where it can only draw air from 90° and it appears to climb even higher. This then heats more surfaces (fuels) through heat transfer, causing a fire to develop with more speed.

We can therefore see how the geometry or shape of a room and the fuel within it affect fire development alongside the availability of oxygen through the air that is contained within the room and the air entering through existing flowpaths, such as open doors, or those created when firefighters open doors without caution or break windows thoughtlessly. All of these actions can affect fire growth.

We have established the basic elements of how a fire grows, and we understand how flames develop and airflows affect growth too. Let's examine the stages of fire development.

The stages of fire development

The development of fire is generally categorised into these stages:

- Initial/incipient

- Developing

- Fully developed (flashover)

- Decay

TEMPERATURE

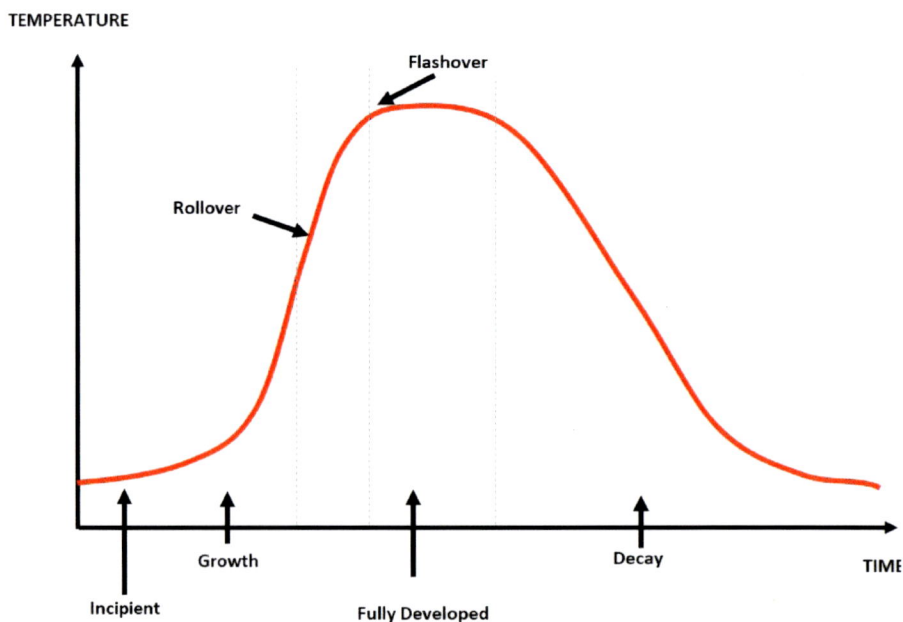

These stages are most often represented by a bell curve

However, this graphic is slightly misleading unless the fire has an unlimited supply of oxygen. The chemical composition of furniture and items with modern compartments has radically altered over the last 20 years. Let's think of the items that are found in houses these days that were not there so long ago.

As I look back on old photos from the 1980s I see many changes, mainly my hairline, but relatively, how little there is in the background of the rooms. On modern photos, despite the absence of hair, there seems to me so much more in terms of furnishing and equipment that could become "fuel" in the event of a fire.

Whilst people use examples such as carbon monoxide with wide flammability limits, we should consider that the mixture of gases released by modern furnishings result in an even wider flammable range, perhaps nearly 90%. Firefighters need to be aware of this and respect this environment in the same they would wading in a pool full of petrol – both could ignite at any moment with devastating effect and tragic consequences.

One of the consequences of modern materials is that they can provide so much fuel that all of the available oxygen in a compartment is soon used up, inhibiting the combustion process. This gives the impression of a 'false decay' – the volume of gas can reduce as the temperature reduces (PVT) leading to the fire appearing to be under control.

It has in fact become a form of 'ventilation controlled' fire, due to its insufficient oxygen supply.

Without the presence of oxygen, heat will still continue to decompose materials and cause 'pyrolysis' and the fuels we mentioned earlier will still be released, but without oxygen. If we look back at our $C^6H^{10}O^5$ formula for wood, if sufficient heat is still present it will continue to pyrolyse and release fuels in chemical/gaseous/vapour form, but there is no longer enough atmospheric oxygen to support burning. As the temperature falls, the extent of this will begin to diminish. As the gases cool, the temperature reduction means the volume reduces and the neutral plane may rise.

The gases produced move above their flammable range. They become too rich to burn. Introduce air (containing oxygen) and they dilute back down into flammable range and the combustion process can start again, except now there are even more fuels in gaseous form in the 3D environment for the firefighter to deal with and the fire can develop even more quickly, perhaps even a rapid fire development which we will cover later.

For these reasons, another bell curve graphic below has been developed which shows this happening.

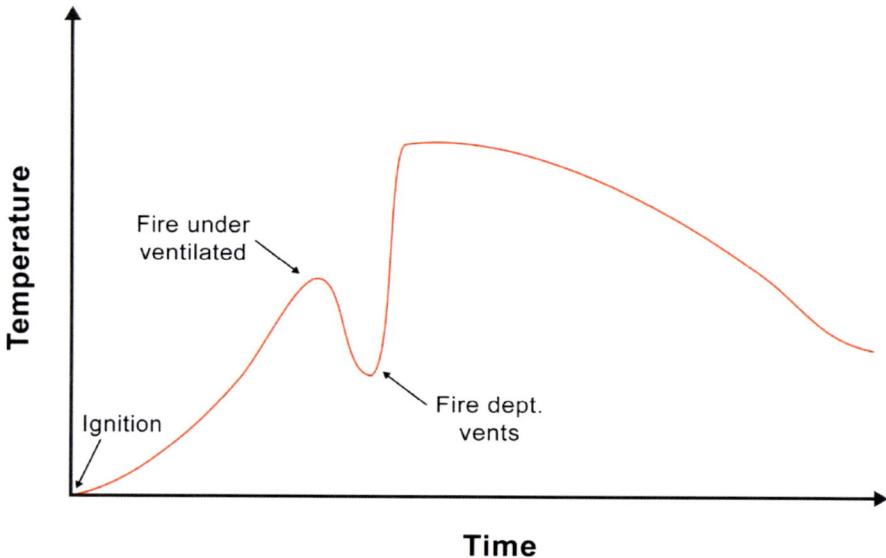

Courtesy of UL/NIST

We can observe the point at which a fire uses up all the available oxygen and the temperature begins to dip, the fire becomes "ventilation controlled", on the graph above it appears to be in "decay", but this is a "false decay", for as soon as the fire department ventilate, or open doors/break windows/roofs creating "inlet flowpaths", providing that source of oxygen, the fire can once again combust and grow.

Note the rapid transition and rate of growth from the point at which ventilation takes place and flowpaths are created by not managing them correctly! This is a situation that we encounter far more often than the first "bell curve".

For firefighters, so how does fire growth affect me?

All of our tactics are governed by the stage of fire growth. If we refer to our operational risk philosophy of risking our lives to save saveable life, risking our lives a little to save saveable property, and not risking our lives at all for deceased lives or unsavable property, then **if we know the stage of growth a fire is at we can make more effective decisions.** If a fire is still in an initial or developing stage, then we may well be able to intervene to save lives and mitigate property damage.

If a fire is fully developed, then the survivability prospects for occupants and structural integrity can be considerably reduced and tactics should be altered accordingly. A fire in decay, where it is certain that all available fuels have been used up may be a slightly safer working environment.

However, we can never be completely certain that we fire gases haven't been forced under pressure into voids and spaces creating pockets of flammable gases. **Or indeed, we can't be sure that the smouldering remains of a fire aren't pyrolyzing and releasing high energy unburned fuels in gaseous forms that are lying in wait for us!**

We must be aware of the stage of fire growth before commencing ventilation operations to prevent worsening conditions. This must be balanced with the positive effects of ventilation which may allow swift rescues to occur. Either way, the growth potential for the fire and its current stage should be evaluated.

When we are moving through a building towards the fire compartment, we should be wary of 'false decay' and be aware that our actions in opening doors en route to the fire can produce flowpaths to feed the fire with oxygen, and that the higher pressures of fire gases can and will move into the areas of lower pressures which we are in. We must have good knowledge and recognition of these conditions and effective ways of controlling the flowpaths we create either through 'door procedures' or other tactics.

In summary

Fire growth is categorised into the following stages:

- Incipient/initial: where the combustion process begins.

- Developing: where the fire accesses further fuel and oxygen allowing it to grow, pyrolysis occurs and fuels in gaseous forms ignite.

- Flashover: the transition phase between developing and fully developed.

- Fully developed: all available fuels are burning with sufficient oxygen supply.

- Decay: fuels are used up and temperatures reduce, combustion ceases.

Remember: fires can present misleading information such as the false decay exhibited by ventilation-controlled fires. Alongside our role as firefighters, we need to also be detectives and work out in seconds what the information is telling us and how our actions can affect it and respond accordingly.

So also, be a Firefighting 'Detective' like Columbo, Magnum P.I., Jim Rockford for the older guys, CSI or Line of Duty for the younger readers and read the signs!

Chapter 4: revision questions

- Describe how the position of a fire in a room affects its growth with examples of a fire in the middle of a room versus a fire in the corner.

- List three items that contribute to the fuel for a compartment fire that were not around 20 years ago.

- What is the effect of these items on fire gas production and flammability limits?

- List the stages of fire growth on a standard bell curve and briefly describe it.

- Which two things are considerably reduced by involvement in a fully developed fire?

- What can firefighters do en-route to the fire compartment to effectively manage flowpaths?

International Compartment Fire Behaviour Training Instructor Course:

This chapter covers the information needed for the following learning outcomes;

Learning Outcome	Description
2.	Understand how fire develops and spreads within compartments
2.1	Explain fire growth in terms of development phases, burning regimes, flashover, backdraft and fire gas ignition (smoke gas explosions)
2.2	Explain the factors which affect the development and spread of a compartment fire including geometry, linings, and fuel package location
2.3	Explain the impact of ventilation openings and the formation of bi-directional and uni-directional flow paths
2.6.	Explain the decay phase in terms of fuel or air depletion

The following videos assist with understanding of this chapter- find them at the YouTube channel: **Ben Walker & Shan Raffel Firefighter Training; tinyurl.com/2xaeb4yu**

Video and Hyperlinks:
Stages of Fire Growth https://tinyurl.com/3mkdksck
Geometry and Location of Fuel Package Affects Fire Development https://tinyurl.com/2jcrba2z
Changes of Ventilation Profile and Effects of Fire https://tinyurl.com/d8v7art4
A Kiwi test of Fire Development and Stages 360 degrees https://tinyurl.com/348z79p2
Fire Growth as seen through a Thermal Image Camera https://tinyurl.com/2vb8jf8x

Speed of fire growth when fully ventilated
https://tinyurl.com/wh38cwwh

Teaching the basics (with more hair). Tyne & Wear Fire & Rescue Service. 2008.

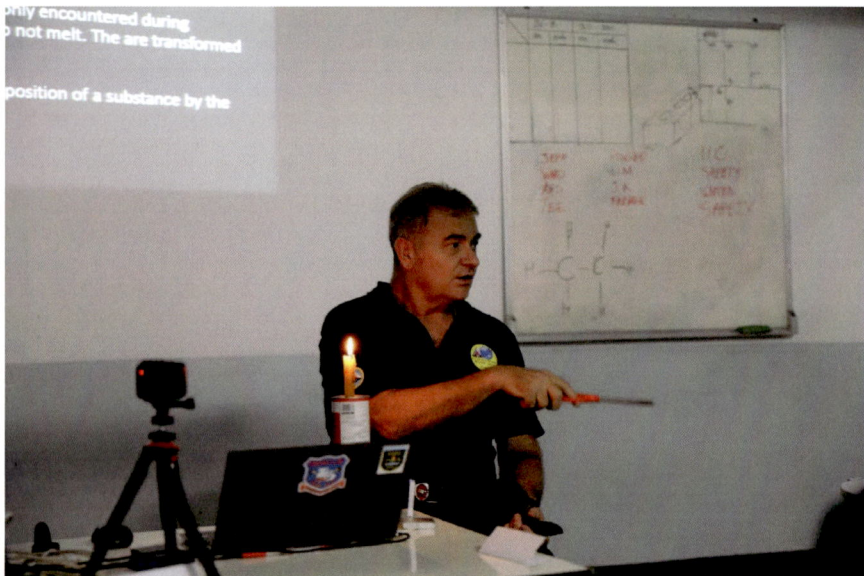

Even a candle can help to understand the fundamentals. CFBT Thailand International CFBT Instructors course 2018.

Chapter 5: Rapid fire developments 1 – flashover

OK, we've covered how fire burns, what it produces, how it happens and what affects it. We also know how it grows, with a little about how that can happen and how our actions sometimes allow it to happen.

For this and subsequent chapters we are going to look in a little more depth at the three following terms and how they happen. This should fill in any gaps from the last chapter.

- Flashover

- Backdraft

- Fire gas ignition

Flashover

For the sake of good form let's start with the official definition of flashover:

'The stage in a ventilated compartment fire where heat from the fire plume, fire gases and compartment boundaries cause the ignition of all exposed combustible surfaces. This sudden & sustained transition to a fully developed fire is "flashover"'

If we look back very briefly at the last chapter on fire growth, you'll remember that flashover is the transition stage between a fire that is developing and a fire that is fully developed – when it has a sufficient and non-exhaustible supply of oxygen to it. So how does this happen? Let's pull together what we already know and find out what causes a 'fire in a room (to) become a room on fire'.

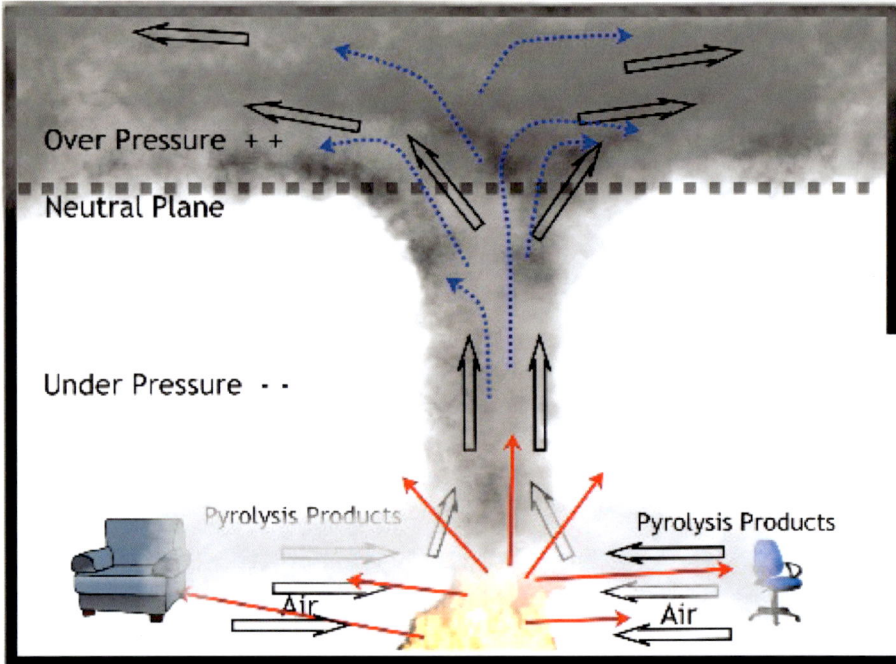

Developing fire (Raffel)

A developing fire is increasing in temperature and heat. The heat causes pyrolysis and the release of fuels in gaseous form (smoke).

Remember PVT and the increased temperature is creating more volume of released gases (fuels), also increasing pressure.

The heat within these gases moves by convection and radiation. Convection is the major heat transfer mechanism. Radiation travels in straight lines and has the greatest impact of objects closest to the fire base.

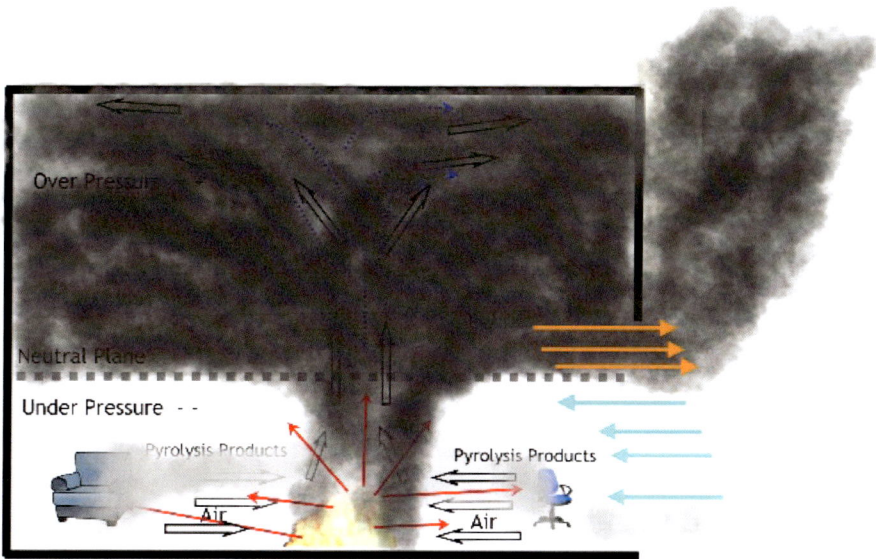

The compartment is filled with super heat unburnt fuel in the smoke layer.

We can see the buoyant released gases, which forms a 'gas layer' at the top of the room. There is a distinct boundary between this buoyant, higher pressure, and less dense cool air beneath.

This boundary or interface of pressures is referred to as the 'neutral plane'. We have a compartment full of gaseous fuels and sufficient oxygen to burn.

When there is a clear separation between these layers, the room is said to be in thermal balance. The temperature at the lower parts of the compartment are significantly lower that the upper layers.

At approximately 600°C the smoke can auto-ignite.

It there is sufficient oxygen available, it is possible for the accumulating unburnt fuel in the smoke to auto-ignite.

Rollover is a term used to describe the movement of the flame front across the ceiling. Often this is not visible in the early stages of the transition and is therefore a very late indicator of impending flashover.

This results in the entire ceiling radiating extreme amounts of heat energy downwards towards the floor.

This rapid rise in temperature usually results in all combustible objects to burn. This causes the bookshelf and its contents, the table, chairs and eventually the carpet to also pyrolyse and contribute gaseous fuel to the fire.

This rapid transitional stage is called flashover

Heat transfer by convection is increased and much of this will flow in the direct of smoke travel to openings, either to atmosphere or into adjacent rooms and voids.

.

Signs and symptoms of flashover

First, let's not beat about the bush: if you're in a room where flashover occurs your chances of survival are very low. Even the best turnout gear gives limited protection. Neither myself, any Compartment Fire Behaviour Instructor, your Chief or your crew mates wants to knock on your wife/partner/parents' door and give them the bad news. I don't want to see any more preventable firefighter line of duty deaths. So please give this your fullest attention.

This list has been around for years, but let's not be guilty of 'list learning' which we all have done at times. Let's think about what we've discussed so far in this book and think about why the signs are happening and what they tell us.

Lowering of the neutral plane

Remember PVT – the temperature is such that the volume of the gases is increasing and moving downwards, this is also accompanied by the rapid temperature increase.

Pyrolysis of all combustible surfaces and pyrolysis at floor level

Two for the price of one here... We know that pyrolysis is caused by heat and that the release of fuel vapours, or 'off-gassing', can be seen. If that's happening everywhere, on all surfaces, we are getting very close to flashover. If it's happening on the carpet or floor, then it is very hot indeed and flashover is imminent.

Fire gas turbulence

Remember the gas flows and the gas laws. As the fire gas increases in temperature and volume it will also increase in pressure, working towards areas of lower pressure. Furniture in rooms, air flowpaths and our actions can also increase the turbulence and surface areas of ignitable fire gases. If these start moving increasingly rapidly it is another sign of impending flashover.

Flames in the gas layer/smoke on fire

Remember the flammable range? Well, the fire gases are well and truly in it and igniting while moving towards areas of lower pressure. The fire is rapidly spreading and moving towards being fully developed.

Rapid increase in temperature

As we know, the radiant heat from the upper gas layer moving down can pyrolyse lower surfaces and increase available fuels. If temperatures increase very quickly this is an indicator of a compartment moving towards flashover. If you start to experience this then you have missed the early indicators an you are in extreme danger. Leave the area immediately!

For firefighters, how can we prevent this?

This is covered in depth in the accompaniment volume to this book in Compartment Firefighting 'Tactics and Techniques' but correct application of water, CAFS and sufficient water flow rates, in conjunction with effective 'flowpath management' can ensure an efficient intervention and successful, safe firefighting, preventing flashover from occurring.

A simple way to think about flashover is that heat is the trigger. For flashover to occur we must have a good supply of air and we must accumulate unburnt fuel in the over pressure zone.

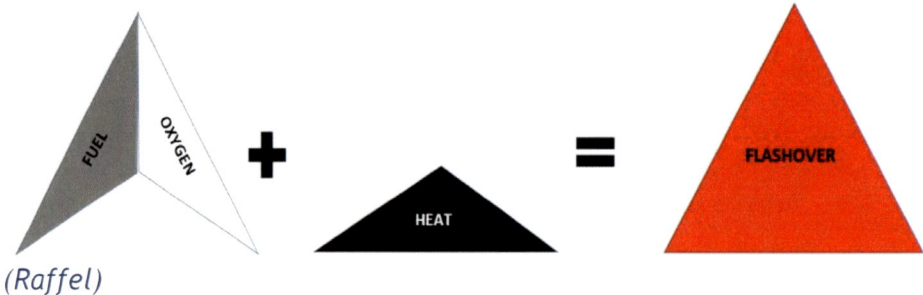

(Raffel)

Chapter 5: Revision questions

- By which method is heat transferred from an upper gas layer to lower areas?

- What is the visible boundary between the areas of high pressure and low pressure in a compartment fire called?

- List and explain signs and symptoms of impending flashover.

- Define flashover in your own words. What is happening? Use diagrams if you like.

International Compartment Fire Behaviour Training Instructor Course: This chapter covers the information needed for the following learning outcomes;

Learning Outcome	Description
1.6	Explain how heat energy can be transferred via conduction, convection and radiation
2.	Understand how fire develops and spreads within compartments
2.1	Explain fire growth in terms of development phases, burning regimes, flashover, backdraft and fire gas ignition (smoke gas explosions)
2.2	Explain the factors which affect the development and spread of a compartment fire including geometry, linings, and fuel package location
2.3	Explain the impact of ventilation openings and the formation of bi-directional and uni-directional flow paths

The following videos assist with understanding of this chapter- find them at the YouTube channel: **Ben Walker & Shan Raffel Firefighter Training;**

Video and Hyperlinks:
Interactive 360 degree house fire from New Zealand Fire & Rescue Service https://tinyurl.com/f9ey5bz8
Flashover Demonstration – Oakridge Fire Dept (USA) https://tinyurl.com/jrvt4dfm
Christmas Tree Flashover https://tinyurl.com/2hbwwr3r
Small Scale Demonstration Flashover https://tinyurl.com/4r2nwcbf

Chapter 6: Rapid fire developments – backdraft

Backdraft. Great movie. I have actually met a couple of retired Chicago Firefighters, stand up Lt Paul Enhelder, who were extras in the film, but I digress...

What is a backdraft?

How does it happen and how can we manage it?

Let's take a look at what we already know.

We have a fire, with heat, oxygen and fuel, but for whatever reason all of the oxygen is used up. This could be because there's a huge ratio of fuel to oxygen, or because flowpaths and air supply to the fire are restricted. So what's happening?

As we know, the heat we've had has caused pyrolysis and we have fuels in gaseous form in the '3D' environment in the compartment. Because these are in an environment without sufficient oxygen they are above the flammable range and too rich to burn.

If we remember PVT; the compartment itself is like a fixed container, so high temperature gases will expand and eventually fill the compartment. When the gases try to expand further they can't due to the boundaries of the compartment, so pressure increases. This is why we see gases forced out of gaps under pressure to areas of lower pressure.

When gases at high temperatures and pressures are forced out, it creates an area of negative pressure inside the fire compartment at a lower level as buoyant gases rise into the space left by gases forced out.

This negative pressure 'draws' or sucks in air at a lower level, which is why an inrush of air can sometimes be felt when opening a door to a backdraft compartment.

While the compartment is generally full of gases, the 'neutral plane' will be at floor level or exceptionally low. According to the rules of PVT, when hot gases are released under pressure and cooler air is drawn in, the temperature is reduced, which also reduces the volume of gas and therefore lifts the neutral plane. As this sucked in air reaches the fire plume (or an area where it was) and is heated naturally, the temperature once again increases, the volume of fire gas increases, and the neutral plane lowers again.

Firefighters should therefore be aware that a 'bouncing' neutral plane can be a sign of backdraft conditions and should consider that any raising of the smoke layer may be due to this rather than effective water application. Don't mistake the two!

A fire that is ventilation controlled doesn't have enough oxygen to burn successfully. It has plenty of fuels in gaseous form, but these are too rich to burn. It may, however, have enough heat to auto-ignite in its flammable range, and it may have enough heat to continue the gaseous fuel production process known as pyrolysis. It certainly has pressure (PVT), and that mass of fuel wants to move to an area of lower pressure.

When an opening is created to a backdraft compartment, air is suddenly reintroduced and dilutes the gases back into their flammable range, rapidly reigniting them. This suddenly increases the temperature in the compartment causing the gases to expand (PVT). This then forces these gases out through the upper part of the opening or, if the pressure is high enough, even to explode through windows etc. As these still unburnt gases exit the compartment, they mix with air outside, also diluting them to within their flammable range and igniting.

We now have a moving mass of gases, in their flammable range, extending from within a compartment to outside, through an opening that has been created.

Note the development of the fire in following figure – the fire is ventilation controlled and although there is a mass of unburned gases (pyrolysis products) there is insufficient oxygen to sustain combustion for long.

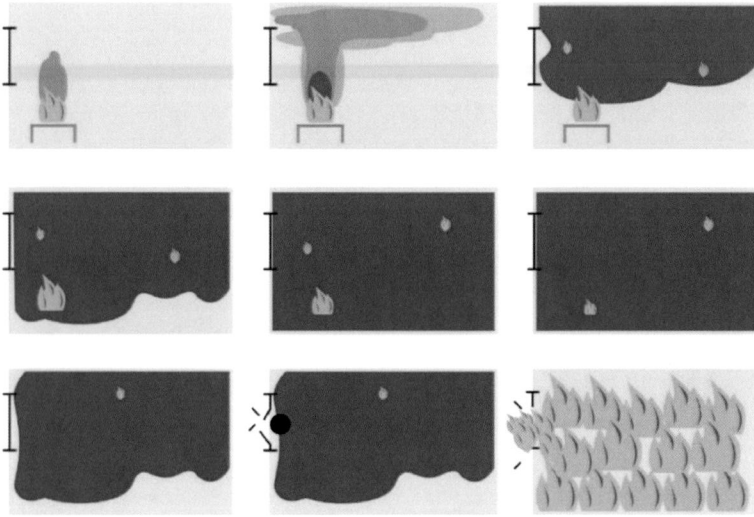

Once the window fails (or is unwittingly broken by a firefighter, or possibly as directed as part of ventilation strategy) then air is drawn in (on the inlet flowpath) dilutes the fire gases to within the flammable range and, with an ignition source or the temperature at auto-ignition levels, the conflagration (flame movement) moves from the higher pressure area to the lower pressure area on the outlet flowpath.

If there is sufficient heat in a compartment, the gases may be at their auto-ignition temperature, and as soon as they dilute into their flammable range they ignite and move through the fuel rapidly from the higher pressure within the compartment to the lower pressures outside of the opening.

Remember- **Auto-Ignition Temperature = A.I.T. (A)** AIR **(I)** IS **(T)** TRIGGER

This flame movement is known as a 'conflagration'. It can be either subsonic (slower than the speed of sound) or supersonic (faster than the speed of sound).

Firefighters can also introduce an ignition to gases that may be at their 'fire-point' but below their 'auto-ignition temperature'.

This can be done by badly-considered water application. For example, forceful jets/streams directed at fuels can agitate embers and ignition sources, knocking them into gaseous fuels in the flammable range and at fire point, acting as a spark to ignite gases and allowing backdraft to occur.

How are openings created?

Openings can be created either through structure failures, such as windows breaking under the heat of gases or by ventilation operations of fire crews, or, more usually, by firefighters opening a door to the under-ventilated compartment where the backdraft lies in wait.

Signs and symptoms of backdraft

As we discussed in Chapter 5 on flashovers, these lists have been around many years, but now we can understand why they happen and what's going on.

Low neutral plane

As we know, although the fire hasn't enough oxygen to burn, it still has heat, causing pyrolysis and releasing gases (PVT) which fill the room. As the room is full, the smoke layer will appear to be exceptionally low or at floor level.

'Bouncing neutral plane'

As gases escape under pressure, heat is released and gas volume reduces (PVT) and the neutral plane rises. As incoming gases are heated, gas volume increases (PVT) and the neutral plane lowers again.

Gases exiting from gaps under pressure

As the volume of gas is constrained by the compartment boundaries, pressure increases as gases can't expand further (PVT). This pressure will force gases out of any small gaps and exits, window frames, door frames and any cavities. This is a classic indicator.

Exiting gases igniting

As above, when these gases exit and mix with air (oxygen) they dilute back into their flammable range. If they are sufficiently hot to be at their auto ignition temperature then they will ignite on exiting. This may well be 'remote' and a short distance from the point of exit.

'Pulsing/Breathing Gases'

We have already explained gases being pushed out of gaps under pressure. As we have also already stated, when this happens it temporarily creates areas of low pressure within the fire compartment which then sucks air in (at a higher pressure) from outside of the compartment. When this happens through the same gaps it appears to be a pulsation or breathing effect. Another classic indicator of impending backdraft.

Inrush of air when opening created (whistling sounds)

When an opening is created, for example by a firefighter opening a door, air is drawn towards the fire by convection currents. This can be felt and seen. It can be accompanied by a whistling sound, though this may be hard to hear when under stress and wearing SCBA.

Turbulent fire gases exiting, alteration in pace, colour and composition

'Mushrooms', 'cauliflowers', 'candy-floss', the alteration reflects the changes in flammability, fuels becoming involved through pyrolysis and turbulence of the gas flow indicating fire growth, increased buoyancy caused by increasing temperatures.

The 'Wedge'

Exiting fire gases under pressure and inrushing air under pressure combine to create an effect that resembles a 'door wedge'. This is a good visual indicator.

Blackened windows

The lack of oxygen means that carbon molecules (C) do not bond with oxygen and as such there a lot of these molecules in a ventilation-controlled fire compartment. As these molecules are adhesive they will adhere, or 'stick' to windows, presenting as soot and blackening windows. The blackened windows are an indicator of a ventilation controlled or oxygen deficient fire.

Definitions of backdraft

To keep the Chiefs happy, let's look at the <u>official definition</u> of a backdraft:

'Limited ventilation can lead to a fire in a compartment producing fire gases containing significant proportions of partial combustion products and unburned pyrolysis products. If these accumulate then the admission of air, when an opening is made to the compartment, can lead to a sudden deflagration. This deflagration moving through the compartment and out of the opening is a backdraft.'

Working definition

'A ventilation-controlled fire situation has developed with quantities of unburned fuels which are pressurised and too rich to burn. Any creation of an opening permits air to enter, gas to exit and gases to dilute into their flammable range. Any ignition source (or AIT) allows combustion to occur and flame movement flows out through the created opening under pressure. This flame movement can be subsonic or supersonic.'

For firefighters, what does backdraft mean to me?

Most fires we now attend will be ventilation controlled due to a number of factors, contents and construction being just two. Therefore, the risk of backdraft is far more frequent now and is a distinct possibility at the majority of compartment fires we attend.

The possibility and frequency of backdraft really highlights the importance of knowing the signs of symptoms and taking appropriate actions, having a working knowledge of how to manage flowpaths, and being able to predict and understand the effect of air on fires when opening doors and windows.

> **So how do we control backdrafts?**
>
> As with flashover, there are certain approaches we can take to dealing with backdraft either by preventing it, or 'inducing' it on our terms. These are covered in detail in the accompaniment "Compartment Firefighting" tactics and techniques.

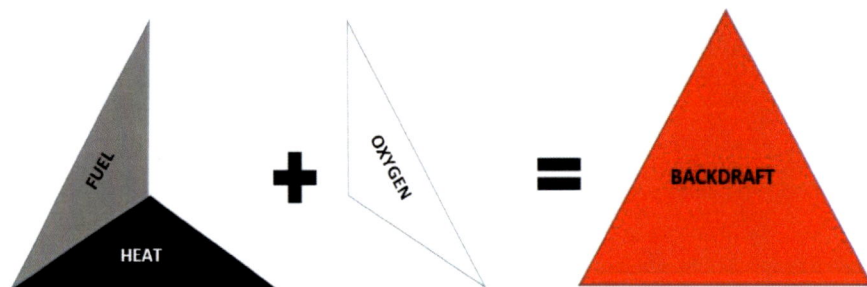

(Raffel)

A simple way of understanding backdraft is to realise that the compartment gases must be in a "too rich" state. Backdraft may be triggered when air is allowed to flow in and dilute the fuel concentration back into a flammable range.

Chapter 6: revision questions

- List two potential ignition sources that may initiate a backdraft.

- What is a 'conflagration'?

- Detail two types of conflagration with reference to their speed.

- What must also be present to create high pressures of fire gas?

- Describe a backdraft in your own words.

- Detail five signs and symptoms that may indicate backdraft conditions.

International Compartment Fire Behaviour Training Instructor Course:

This chapter covers the information needed for the following learning outcomes;

Learning Outcome	Description
1.3	Explain complete combustion, incomplete combustion and passive agents
1.4	Describe flammable limits and the impact of variations in temperature and pressure.
1.7	1.7 Explain extinguishing principles in terms of actions that can disrupt the chemical reaction by removing one of more of the sides of the fire triangle
2.	Understand how fire develops and spreads within compartments
2.1	Explain fire growth in terms of development phases, burning regimes, flashover, backdraft and fire gas ignition (smoke gas explosions)
2.2	Explain the factors which affect the development and spread of a compartment fire including geometry, linings, and fuel package location
2.3	Explain the impact of ventilation openings and the formation of bi-directional and uni-directional flow paths
2.5	Explain fire spread through multi compartment structures
2.6.	Explain the decay phase in terms of fuel or air depletion
3.	Understand the tactics, tools and techniques used by firefighters to deal with and prevent fire development within a compartment

The following videos assist with understanding of this chapter- find them at the YouTube channel: **Ben Walker & Shan Raffel Firefighter Training;** tinyurl.com/2xaeb4yu

Video and Hyperlinks:
4k HD Ultra Slow Motion Backdraft https://tinyurl.com/3ekscjad
Slow Motion Backdraft Container https://tinyurl.com/n89zuh34
Backdraft Simulation https://tinyurl.com/yfzk5x32
Signs and Symptoms of Backdraft https://tinyurl.com/sb8n6z
Backdraft Compilation https://tinyurl.com/2m6hn6hx

Chapter 7: Rapid fire developments – Fire Gas Ignition

Fire Gas Ignition (FGI) is perhaps the most misinterpreted and misunderstood of the rapid-fire developments. In our discussion on flashover and backdraft we have defined events that occur in the fire involved compartment. FGI is a phenomenon in which fire gases in the flammable range have accumulated in a compartment that is remote to the compartment that the fire is in.

This can be caused by smoke traveling through ducting or ventilation systems, and also heat from a fire compartment causing pyrolysis of adjacent compartments' elements. For example, the heat generated in a fire in a room below may cause the floor and carpets in the room above to pyrolyse and release the gaseous fuels into the compartment.

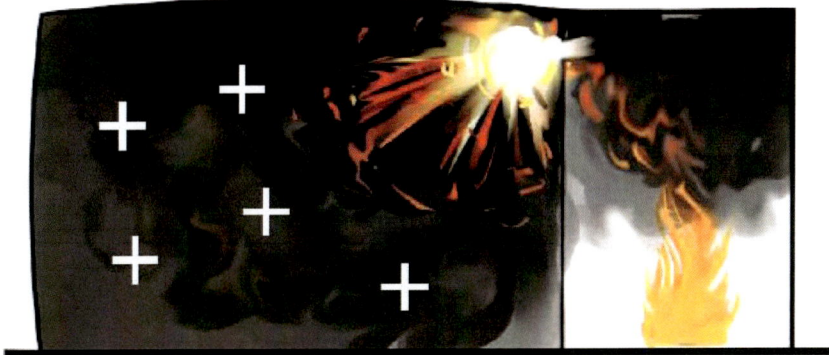

An example of travel in a domestic property fire is provided in the following figure. Note that the pilot light oven in the second compartment will act as an ignition source for accumulated gases which have mixed with the air in the second compartment to dilute into their flammable range. The nearer this ratio is to its ideal mixture (or 'stoichiometric mix') the greater the force of ignition shall be.

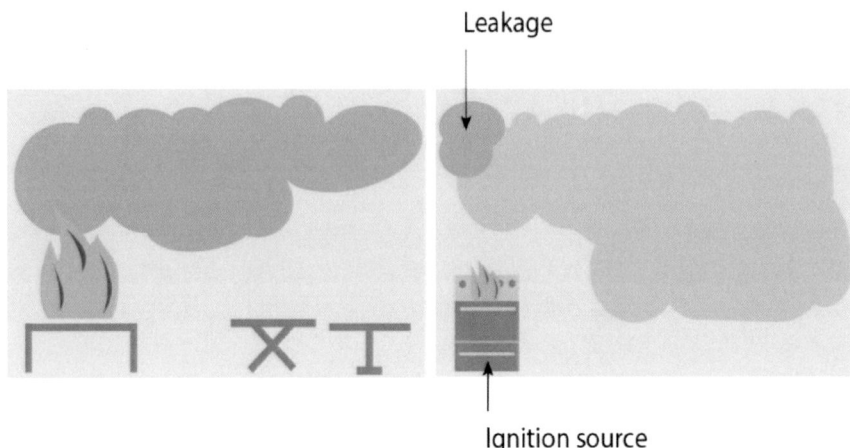

Leakage

Ignition source

FGI from pilot light

As with a backdraft, all that is required is an ignition source to ignite these gases, and similarly, this can be created by both failure of structural elements such as the fire breaking through the floor to ignite accumulated fire gases in the room above, or the actions of firefighters, particularly uncontrolled ventilation operations which may cause fires to 'climb' and break into the compartments where the fire gas has accumulated.

PVT can be applicable to fire gas ignition compartments. If the fire gases have been released due to pyrolysis rather than from travelling from the fire compartment, then there is a clear indicator that high temperatures are affecting the compartment. If these are at floor level then it identifies the location of the fire to firefighters.

Effective use of thermal image cameras can really assist in identifying fire location and indicating that we may be operating in a situation where fire gas ignition can occur.

Referring back to our PVT gas laws and the buoyancy of heated gas, a classic area for accumulation of fire gases remote to the compartment of fire origin are roof voids. I actually have seen this myself at a fire in Gateshead, England.

Fire gas ignitions can be accompanied by pressure waves and, like backdrafts, pressurised gases will move from areas of higher pressure to lower pressure. They can be subsonic or supersonic. A subsonic fire gas ignition may burn itself out fairly quickly, using up all the fuel such as a fuel at 'flash point'. That is why these are sometimes referred to as 'flash-fires'. The Gateshead fire gas ignition I experienced was an example of this. From the command post I witnessed a flash and a large 'clap' sound, followed by nothing. Fortunately, no firefighters were in the roof void at the time.

Fire gas ignitions can also become detonations, moving supersonically – faster than the speed of sound. A tragic example of this is the fatal fire in Blaina, South Wales, in 1996. A huge pressure wave accompanied a fire gas ignition which detonated, causing 'blast injuries', fatally wounding two firefighters. The force of the pressure wave was such that it forced doors shut, 'crimping' high pressure hose reel tubing and hampering all subsequent rescue attempts.

These high-pressure deflagrations are sometimes referred to as 'smoke explosions'.

For firefighters, what do fire gas ignitions mean for me?

The most important thing to learn from fire gas ignition is, again, the importance of remembering that we are operating in a 3D environment. At all times. This remains the case when we know that the fire is in another part of the building. We may even think that it is contained, but the dangerous, flammable fire gases may have travelled, leaving us in an environment full of fuel, just awaiting an ignition source.

We do operate in areas away from the compartment where the fire is located or is known to be. Search sectors are set up on floors above and in different parts of the building. What happens if we enter a room where there is no fire but it is full of fire gas? This indicates that the fire is spreading, gases are accumulating and we are at risk.

It shows the importance of having extinguishing media with us at all times when operating within any area of the risk, to be able to effectively deal with this.

Signs and symptoms of fire gas ignition

Accumulation of fire gases/smoke in a compartment known to be remote from the fire compartment

This can be caused by 'travel', a possible indicator of hidden fire spread.

Indication of heat from floors/walls/ceilings in rooms with no fire

Using a thermal image camera in these circumstances gives a good indicator of the fire location and presents safety critical information. Floors may be weakened structurally by direct fire impingement, for example. Extreme caution should be taken. But remember, FGI is still possible even if the temperature of the area where smoke is collecting is relatively low.

Pyrolysis of any surface and those near, or that are, compartment boundaries

Pyrolysis of surfaces is an indicator of fuel being released into the compartment. Although it may not yet be 'smoke filled' or contain plentiful fire gas, this is a classic indication of a situation that will develop. To prevent this, another crew has to address the heat in the other compartment that is causing the pyrolysis.

Definitions of fire gas ignition

The official definition is as follows:

'Any accumulation of unburned fuels, pyrolysis products in a compartment remote from that of fire origin. Once within the flammable range, given the introduction of an ignition source, these will ignite and deflagrate either sub or supersonically.'

Two working definitions:

'A build-up of gaseous fuels in an area away from the fire compartment that mixed with air and an ignition source will ignite with varying force.'

'An ignition of accumulated fire gases and combustion products, existing in, or transported into, a flammable state'

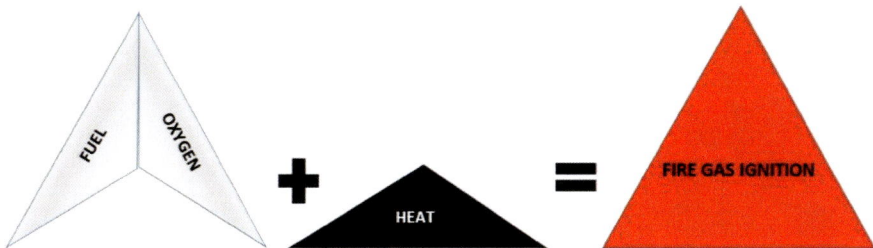

(Raffel)

A simple way of understanding FGI is to understand that smoke that is laden with unburnt fuel can migrate away from the original fire compartment. In the process there will be a degree of "pre-mixing" with air. An ignition source introduced to this mixture may result in a very sudden and powerful event.

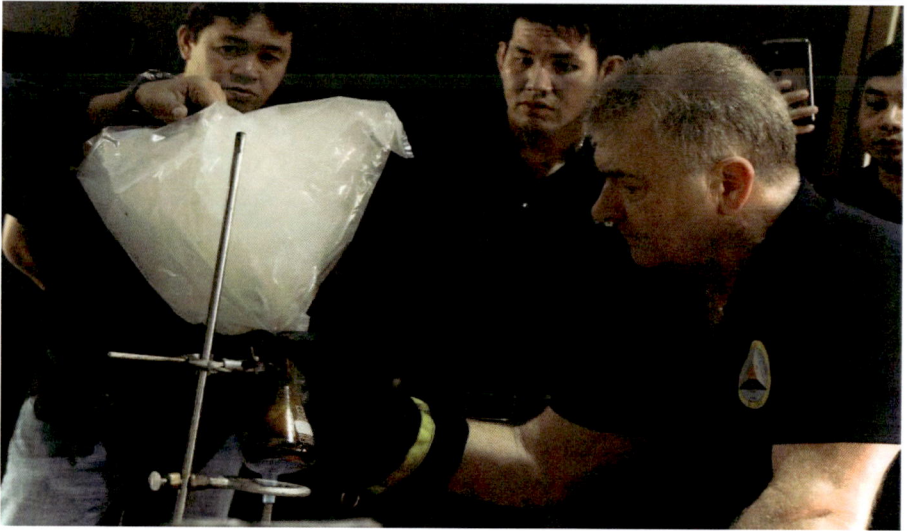

Shan Raffel captures the white cold smoke from a flask where wood chips are pyrolyzing. A lighter is used to ignite the "smoke" and it is rapidly transformed to flame.

Chapter 7: revision questions

- How can fire gas accumulate in a compartment remote from the fire?
- What is a fire gas ignition? Explain using your own words.
- Detail signs and symptoms of fire gas ignition.
- If heat is displayed at floor level on a thermal image camera, what does that indicate?
- Fire gas ignitions are sometimes referred to as both 'flash fires' and 'smoke explosions' - differentiate between the two.

International Compartment Fire Behaviour Training Instructor Course:

This chapter covers the information needed for the following learning outcomes;

Learning Outcome	Description
1.3	Explain complete combustion, incomplete combustion and passive agents
1.4	Describe flammable limits and the impact of variations in temperature and pressure
2	Understand how fire develops and spreads within compartments
2.1	Explain fire growth in terms of development phases, burning regimes, flashover, backdraft and fire gas ignition (smoke gas explosions)
2.2	Explain the factors which affect the development and spread of a compartment fire including geometry, linings, and fuel package location
2.5	Explain fire spread through multi compartment structures
2.6	Explain the decay phase in terms of fuel or air depletion
3	Understand the tactics, tools and techniques used by firefighters to deal with and prevent fire development within a compartment

The following videos assist with understanding of this chapter- find them at the YouTube channel: **Ben Walker & Shan Raffel Firefighter Training;**

Video and Hyperlinks:
Fire Gas Ignition - Differences https://tinyurl.com/hap6663m
Fire Gas Ignition- Model from above https://tinyurl.com/h4abse2r
French Fire Gas Ignitions https://tinyurl.com/durd9skz
The best FGI video – low temperature smoke is still highly flammable fuel! https://tinyurl.com/895xs82e

Chapter 8: Rapid fire developments – blowtorch, wind driven and external spread fires

In the UK we have sadly lost four firefighters in two fires at high rise buildings over the last ten years. At both of these incidents, environmental factors were not fully accounted for, and wind particularly had an effect on the fire dynamics. Let's take a closer look.

Wind is a feature at all types of fires, from the wildfires moving through vegetation to structure fires. As height increases the effects of wind are often amplified. Weather and wind patterns are extremely complex meteorological concepts, but what does it mean for us?

We have repeated our PVT mantra and again return to it. If air (wind) is blown into a room with no other openings then the pressure rises proportionally to the wind speed. The room will pressurise. If a door is open (creating a flowpath), the room will still pressurise, albeit more slowly, and there will be a flow of air between the inlet and the open door (outlet).

As we discussed earlier, a turbulent gas flow (created by the wind and mixing with the fire gases) can result in faster flame speeds and fire spread. With additional wind producing a better mixing environment for fuel, it can optimise conditions for more complete combustion (everything is burning). When these conditions exist, fuel is used more quickly, has a greater heat release rate and higher temperatures.

So, with the introduction of wind, we have more heat energy being released, faster flame speeds and higher temperatures. Each is dangerous enough on its own.

How does wind get introduced and what then happens?

A common cause of wind introduction is the failure of windows caused by heat. If a window has failed in an environment with no wind, then there will be a visible neutral plane as fire gas under pressure leaves the upper portion and air is drawn in through the lower portion of the opening. This is referred to as our 'bi-directional flowpath'.

Look at the following figure. In a situation where there is no wind and the window at the bottom of the diagram fails, then we see the bi-directional flowpath – hot fire gases exiting with external air being drawn in.

If a fire crew then creates an exit outlet, in this case a ceiling vent, then it creates an additional flowpath. There is fire gas exhausting from the window, but the majority is flowing through the building towards ceiling vent.

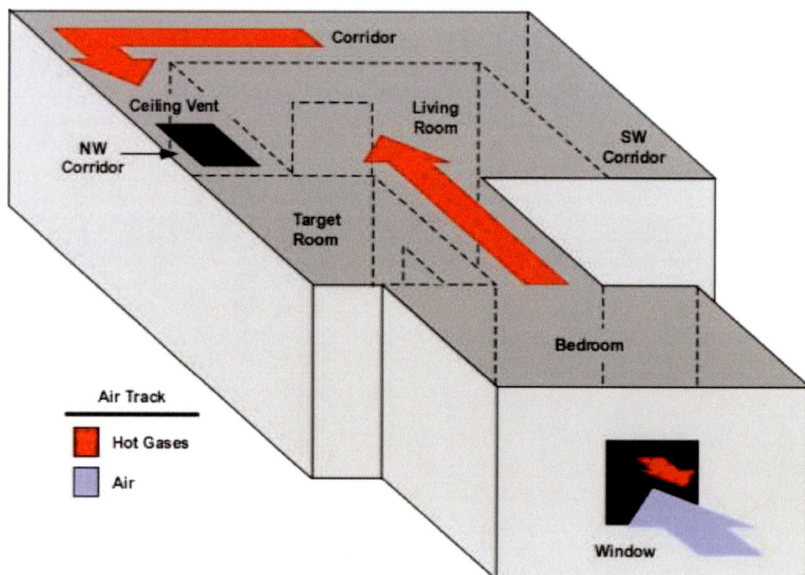

Credit LA County FD

With the addition of wind there is a 'sealing effect' at the inlet which prevents fire gases from exiting the window, meaning all of the fire gas flows towards the ceiling vent. The bi-directional flow has been replaced by a single or 'unidirectional' flow. (Entering air travels along inlet flowpath to fire, hot gases travel along outlet flowpath to exit vent.) When the wind is introduced to flowpaths that have definitive inlet and exit routes, a unidirectional flow can move, filling all space along that route. Particularly in high rise, multi-occupancy buildings there may be corridors which have a 'channelling' effect. This flowpath of fire can be referred to as a 'blowtorch' effect due to its speed of travel, high temperatures and heat release rate.

For firefighters, what does this mean?

As previously mentioned, once wind is introduced to a completed flowpath then the blowtorch effect can occur. It is of the utmost importance that we consider the following priorities when we suspect or know we are battling wind-driven fire conditions.

We have to be vigilant not to create a completed flowpath (creating an exhaust vent/outlet) which we have to get between to advance towards the fire (we won't be able to). Controlling doors, windows and managing flowpaths must be treated as a risk critical priority!

As we have also said, wind driven fires generate fast, efficient, high temperature combustion with high heat release rates. Therefore, we need sufficient flow rates to effectively control and extinguish fires. We need to ensure sufficient and continuous water supplies before mounting any attack.

Signs and symptoms of wind-driven fires

On arrival, use landmarks to check for wind direction and speed (flags, trees, windsocks, dust).

Broken/open windows

Firefighters should consider potential and existing flowpaths.

Broken windows known to be on the upwind side, where flames may be visible but fire gases are not exiting [Bold]

If we see no bi-directional flow, it indicates the wind has 'sealed' the inlet and created a single flowpath into the compartment/building.

Large flames/gases on the downwind side

The laws of pressure suggest that the gases want to escape but are also being forced by the wind pressure. Imagine trying to spray water out of your mouth. Now try doing it with a tailwind. You will still be able to spit/spray some out, but it will travel further and more dramatically with the wind assistance!

Pressurised smoke escaping from gaps in closed doors/windows on the potential outlet flow path towards exhaust vents/outlet

This suggests a pressurised situation has already occurred with the potential to create a unidirectional flowpath once the door is opened or vent created.

'Pulses' or 'belches' of smoke from the upwind window

Pulsing or belching smoke from an upwind window is an indicator that a compartment is pressurised to such an extent that it cannot release all of the pressure to an exhaust vent (a complete flowpath has not yet been created), so in effect is 'belches' out to release pressure.

While the signs and symptoms of wind-driven fires and indications of potentially dangerous situations are similar to indicators for other rapid fire developments, the environment and building we operate in should be our biggest indicator, and it should it vital to remember that high rise buildings lend themselves especially well to the possibility of wind-driven, rapidly developing fire situations.

The Coanda effect

The Coanda effect is a fluid dynamics principle that is defined as 'the tendency of a fluid jet to be attracted to a nearby surface'

If we look at the following figure based upon Mark Fishlock's work, we can see that exiting gases cannot escape and are drawn back against the building's surface. This allows heat to be transferred via convection to materials on the surfaces above such as windows, which may fail and allow fire spread into compartments above the initial fire floor. It facilitates vertical fire travel in this instance.

In addition to this, the proliferation of aluminium composite panels (ACPs) also known as "cladding" can add fuel to a fire. The Coanda effect draws heat back to the building and can cause the insulated core (unless inert materials are used) of these panels to heat, pyrolyse and become involved in the fire.

If the fire spreads into the cavity between the building and the inside of the panel, the flames can only draw air from a limited radius, so will extend considerably, causing more pyrolysis and flame spread.

This can lead to a "full height, external spread fire" as noted at The Torch building fire in Dubai, Grenfell Tower in London, Lacrosse Building in Melbourne, Grozny City Towers in Chechnya, Monte-Carlo Hotel in Las Vegas, USA, Garnock Court in Scotland, UK.

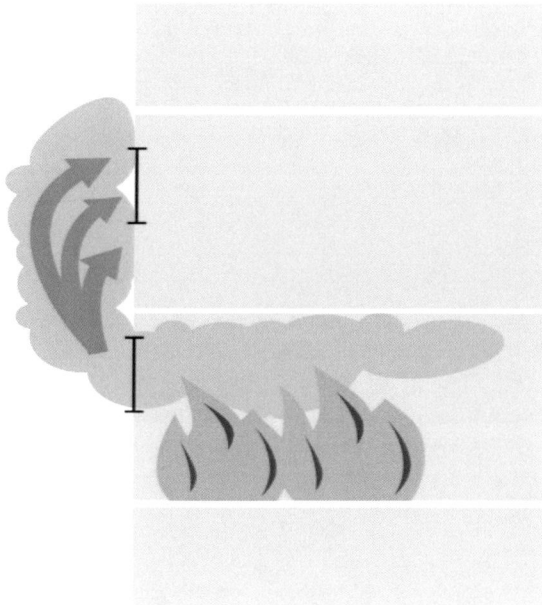

The Coanda effect draws hot gases back towards the building.

Chapter 8: revision questions

- What happens to a room proportional to wind speed when an inlet is created?
- List three effects on a fire when wind creates optimal mixing conditions for fuel and air.
- What must firefighters be vigilant not to do when attending wind-driven fires?
- Name three things firefighters can look at to assess wind direction and speed when arriving on scene.
- Briefly explain the difference between a 'bi-directional' and 'uni-directional flowpath'.
- List three signs and symptoms that a wind-driven fire may be in progress.

International Compartment Fire Behaviour Training Instructor Course:

This chapter covers the information needed for the following learning outcomes;

Learning Outcome	Description
2	2. Understand how fire develops and spreads within compartments
2.2	2.2 Explain the factors which affect the development and spread of a compartment fire including geometry, linings, and fuel package location
2.3	2.3 Explain the impact of ventilation openings and the formation of bi-directional and uni-directional flow paths
2.4	2.4 Explain the impact of a Wind Driven fire on the heat release rate
2.5	2.5 Explain fire spread through multi compartment structures
2.6	2.6. Explain the decay phase in terms of fuel or air depletion
3	3. Understand the tactics, tools and techniques used by firefighters to deal with and prevent fire development within a compartment
3.1	3.1 Explain offensive/internal attack, transitional attack, and defensive/external attack strategies

| 3.2 | 3.2 Identify nozzle techniques that may be suited to internal attack, transitional attack and external attack |
| 3.3 | 3.3 Explain ventilations tactics and techniques that can be synergistically combined with various nozzle techniques |

The following videos assist with understanding of this chapter- find them at the YouTube channel: **Ben Walker & Shan Raffel Firefighter Training;** **tinyurl.com/2xaeb4yu**

Video and Hyperlinks:
Time Lapse Dubai External Fire Spread https://tinyurl.com/xe6z8c74
High Rise Building External Spread Fire https://tinyurl.com/622c8ka6
External Building Cladding and Fires https://tinyurl.com/94v3yu6u
Wind-driven fire research https://tinyurl.com/tz9mxtp9
Exterior Conditions of Wind-driven fires https://tinyurl.com/tjzszwjp
Wind-driven fire- NIST, Chicago, USA https://tinyurl.com/myf83fk7
Firefighting Tactics in Wind-driven fires part 1 https://tinyurl.com/bcbxbuty
Firefighting Tactics in Wind-driven fires part 2 https://tinyurl.com/8ae9sdc
Attacking Wind-driven fires with a "floor-below" nozzle https://tinyurl.com/4669kax2
Chimney and Trench Effect https://tinyurl.com/k6evrbcb
King's Cross Fire- Trench Effect https://tinyurl.com/5t3upbh8

Positive Pressure Ventilation is a great tool and, used correctly, can be extremely effective. But it cannot overcome wind speeds of over 6MPH. Tyne & Wear Fire & Rescue Service. 2011.

Chapter 9: Effect of building and construction on fire dynamics

The effects of building construction on fire dynamics is a very complex subject that many finer minds than our own work on diligently. As before, we are going to look at some basic concepts that may keep us safer on the incident ground.

We have previously seen how the shape (geometry) of the fuel package, it's location, and the availability of air flow and the available exhaust path can affect the rate of fire development. So how does the compartment size and structure affect fire dynamics?

Large compartments

I think we can all accept that smaller rooms with sufficient oxygen and available fuels will reach flashover more quickly than larger rooms, as, put simply, in larger rooms there are more contents to pyrolyse, radiant heat needs to be generated over a larger area and there is more volume for fire gases to expand into.

In large buildings with large, relatively empty, compartments and high ceilings there will be more available air in the room to begin with that will support combustion, and it may therefore take a lot longer until a fire reaches a ventilation-controlled stage, if indeed it does at all.

There may be a lower ratio of fuel to air in ballrooms, assembly halls and auditoriums, for example, and this may take fire gases out of their flammable range and become 'too lean to burn' in certain areas, while they remain within their flammable range in other areas.

While it may be true that ventilation-controlled situations may seldom arise in the early stages of fires in warehouses and storage centres etc., we may still have copious fuels available that can contribute to a massive heat release rate and a rapidly developing fire.

- Larger volumes of compartment will require a larger volume of fire gas to fill before starting to become pressurised.
- External signs such as gases being pushed through gaps under pressure may not be exhibited.
- Gases will also be present in different concentrations (flammability limits) in different areas in the compartment.

Hot fire gases may reach a certain height (below the ceiling) where they start to cool, lose volume and buoyancy, and start to sink back towards floor level. There is therefore less opportunity for heat to transfer horizontally across ceilings (convection) and to radiate back into the compartment. Indeed, there is much further to travel.

Because of these factors, the rate of fire growth in large compartments may be slower, and firefighters may be making entry at differing stages of fire development in contrast to a domestic dwelling fire. A firefighter may be entering 'pre-flashover', in a developing stage, which can potentially be more dangerous than a house fire which may have started to go into decay having used all available fuels.

In larger commercial buildings there is more likelihood of the existence of heating and ventilation systems, ducting and pipework which provides opportunities for hidden fire spread and travel.

Warehouses and storage facilities may contain such large quantities of potential fuels that, combined with the large amount of air (oxygen) already present, there is potential for extremely high temperatures, heat release rates and speed of development. If we consider the construction of warehouses, if cladded panels fail, there can be huge inlets, drawing in air, possibly wind driven, and we have all the ingredients for a recipe for disaster.

Without failure of elements, supermarkets and warehouses with racking can cause a 'compartmentalising' effect, acting like walls and allowing radiant heat to contribute to fire growth. It is not out of the question that we can have smaller areas of 'localized flashover' within larger compartments.

Artificial corridors/aisles created by racking can also create an effect like a corridor or pipe, creating a flowpath with less resistance, allowing fire and gases to travel along its route to the outlet/exhaust vent.

Structures of larger compartments may be more likely, or even designed, to fail and collapse. Exposed steel beams and columns, for example, lose two thirds of their integrity at 693°c, so structural collapse is a real risk, while public centres such as shopping centres/malls, sports arenas and concert halls may have atriums with fixed 'fail' ventilation points as part of a "fire engineered building design".

These can alter the fire dynamics. Let's remember that the point of this type of fire safety design is to release smoke/fire gas to let members of the public escape from potentially dangerous situations over a calculated time scale.

Firefighters will be responding and making entry in the time period after this window has expired and are now dealing with a fire that is at least partially ventilated and flowpaths have possibly been created.

Multiple inlets/outlets can cause turbulent gas flows, which as we know can increase the speed and intensity of fire development, presenting another hazard.

For firefighters, what does this mean?

If we are operating offensively inside a large warehouse, we should be cautious of differing fire dynamics in different areas of the compartment, and the different stages of fire development in different areas of large compartments. These can be termed 'travelling fires'. We have less control of doors, but must still consider flow paths and the potential for wind-driven and blowtorch effects along flowpaths/channels created by aisles and racking.

We are still operating in a '3D' environment with lots of space for gaseous fuels to accumulate and potentially get behind us, cutting off our egress. We may also find that, as we progress, a localised area within the warehouse starts behaving like a smaller compartment.

Firefighters have to remain exceptionally vigilant at fires in larger compartments as there are many more variables that cannot be controlled compared to fires in dwellings or smaller compartments, and these considerations and the effect on fire dynamics should be reviewed continually.

Factors to consider

- Contents and fuel package affecting fire development and potential.

- Creation of artificial flowpaths by racking/aisles with potential for blowtorch effects.

- Compartmentalising effects with potential for localised flashover and rapid developments.

- Fire gases at different concentrations and flammability throughout the compartment

- Fire development at different stages throughout large compartments

- Availability of air is greater due to volume of building/compartment so the stage of fire growth may be different to that encountered normally as it has not become ventilation controlled.

- Fixed installations (heating ventilation ducting etc.) can induce hidden fire spread and allow fire gases to travel to other areas of the compartment.

- Fire safety designs can contribute by creating multiple flowpaths as well as areas of negative pressure which can have a 'drawing' effect on a fire. A classic example of this can be where a pressurised enclosed stairwell also has a vent at the top of the shaft. The vertically rising airflow (flowpath) of fresh air inputted by the system that pressurises the stairwell then creates a 'flue' with areas of negative pressure created as it passes each horizontal floor. As we know (PVT) buoyant and pressurised fire gases will move to these areas of lower pressure and are sucked towards the stairwell, which may well be the point of our 'Bridgehead' or 'Forward Command Post'.

Heritage properties

Pre-20th century buildings, and also certain 20th century buildings, can affect fire dynamics. If we look at the materials in heritage properties such as old libraries, museums, castles, stately homes, the contents may be dryer and less humid in order to preserve them. With less moisture in the fuel, less water vapour and carbon dioxide is released to act as passive agents and absorb energy to slow fire development. As you may expect, this can lead to faster developing fires with fuel conditions that contribute to effective combustion.

However, the opposite can also be true. Heritage properties can also be damp and therefore have more water based pyrolysis products acting as passive agents and slowing the fire development.

Buildings such as former bonded warehouses, distilleries and manufacturing plants present specific risks. Materials such as

alcohols, solvents and chemicals may have impregnated or been absorbed into the linings such as walls and floors over a number of years, and in a fire situation release numerous chemical combinations forming gaseous fuels. This can seriously impact on the speed of fire development.

Courtesy of The Independent. December 2015.

Heritage properties have a number of potential effects on fire behavior and traditional construction increases potential for collapses.
Note here how the windows have all become potential inlets, affecting the ventilation profile of the fire and increasing the potential for turbulent gas flows. This makes interior attack/compartment firefighting extremely challenging and hazardous.

Ben's former colleagues have opted here for defensive/exterior attack in this case, using an aerial ladder platform as a 'water tower'.

Commercial premises

As we covered earlier, available fuels in the home have altered dramatically over the last 20 years. This is applicable to commercial premises. As all businesses become more reliant on technology, these buildings contain far more electrical equipment such as computers, computer servers, and possibly fixed fire installations beyond that of water sprinklers.

Offices and "Server Rooms" may contain carbon dioxide, nitrogen or even halon release systems to suppress the combustion process by releasing these gases in a fixed volume container 'sealed room' to create and oxygen deficient environment and prevent combustion. While this may well be effective, there is the possibility of disrupting that intervention when we create flowpaths and negate the effect of the fixed suppression system, creating conditions for fire while up close and personal.

Even without the fixed installations, the amount of technology that is found will release heat energy quickly and use up available oxygen creating ventilation controlled situations. Should any failure of an element occur, existing ventilation and heating systems spread the fire, or fire service interventions might create a supply of oxygen (flowpath) leading to rapid fire developments.

Chapter 9: revision questions

- What will fires in larger volume compartments have a large supply of?

- What is the potential effect on flammability limits of large compartments?

- Which building design features can induce hidden fire spread?

- Detail two potential effects on fire behavior that heritage properties may have?

- In a 20 storey building, if we create a vertical flowpath of fresh air entering the bottom of a stairwell and exiting through an exhaust vent on the top of the stairwell. What effect will that have on a fire on the 8th floor?

- List three factors to consider at fires in larger compartments.

<u>International Compartment Fire Behaviour Training Instructor Course:</u>

This chapter covers the information needed for the following learning outcomes;

Learning Outcome	Description
1.3	Explain complete combustion, incomplete combustion and passive agents
1.4	Describe flammable limits and the impact of variations in temperature and pressure.
1.5	Explain the chemistry of combustion in solids, liquids, gases, dusts and vapour phases
1.6	Explain how heat energy can be transferred via conduction, convection and radiation
1.7	Explain extinguishing principles in terms of actions that can disrupt the chemical reaction by removing one of more of the sides of the fire triangle
2	Understand how fire develops and spreads within compartments

2.1	Explain fire growth in terms of development phases, burning regimes, flashover, backdraft and fire gas ignition (smoke gas explosions)
2.2	Explain the factors which affect the development and spread of a compartment fire including geometry, linings, and fuel package location
2.3	Explain the impact of ventilation openings and the formation of bi-directional and uni-directional flow paths

The following videos assist with understanding of this chapter- find them at the YouTube channel: **Ben Walker & Shan Raffel Firefighter Training;** tinyurl.com/2xaeb4yu

Video and Hyperlinks:
Lightweight Type Domestic Construction Fire https://tinyurl.com/3vfrmawm
Lightweight Type Construction Fire Failures https://tinyurl.com/x9vk49tx
Complete Combustion in European Type Construction https://tinyurl.com/f2y66bpx
"Station" Nightclub, Warwick, Rhode Island, USA https://tinyurl.com/v28f3cw

Chapter 10: Water application

Water application is perhaps the most misinterpreted, misunderstood and misapplied aspect of Compartment Fire Behaviour Training. And I am going to say it:

It is not all about 'pulsing'

Indeed, one of my esteemed mentors, Bill Gough, former Principal Officer of the West Midlands Fire Service in the UK and International General Assembly Chair of the IFE, goes even further, suggesting that inappropriate gas cooling at the wrong time with low flows is costing lives. And he has a point – pulsing, or pulsation, is a technique to be deployed when appropriate. It is a tool to control gases and move to a position where we can extinguish the fire.

For the extrication aficionados among us, you wouldn't do a 'dashboard roll' at an RTC/MVA if it required a 'roof fold down' would you?

Ok, now I've 'crossed the Rubicon'...

The simplest way to reduce the risk presented by a fire is to put it out, extinguish it, get the wet stuff on the red stuff. The risk of rapid-fire developments, structural collapse and other hazards reduce if we reduce the exposure time by extinguishing the fire as soon as we safely can. Note that sentence well: *as soon as we safely can.*

Get the fire out, reduce the other risks.

'we should always remember that the best way to accomplish the rescue objective is to take the danger away from the victims or put out the fire. Even if the fire is not immediately controlled or extinguished, a quick attack can slow the spread of the fire and buy other firefighters additional time to take the victims away from the danger'.
R Hiraki - Assistant Chief Seattle WA

We need to look at getting the fire out, and this requires us to extinguish the 'fuel bed'. But we need to consider the 3D environment that the pyrolysis products and gaseous fuels released from the fuels create. So, what are our options? These are covered in depth in our book "Fighting Fire"

Methods include:

- Direct cooling

- Indirect cooling

- Gas cooling

Let's look at each of these in turn.

Direct application

Direct application is a method in which a firefighter applies water from the nozzle directly onto/into the surfaces of materials that are on fire – the fuel bed. If a fire is accessible than this is going to be the quickest way of putting it out. However, we could still have gaseous fuels (smoke) on fire and our water stream will entrain air that "feeds" the fire too, so it may not address the risks completely. It may also generate significant quantities of steam which will move towards areas of lower pressure (PVT) along any flowpaths that are in existence or have been created. Steam burns are not fun.

Let's take one of Ben's own experience as an example. As a young probationary firefighter in a busy metropolitan department in North East England (think Pittsburgh /Cleveland /Detroit), I attended a fire in a basement. Making our way down the stairs, we opened the door creating what we know now as a bi-directional flowpath (same inlet and outlet).

The 'old hand' Trevor said to me in his Northern Irish accent, *'Get low, get inside and away from the door, use the light of the fire and have a quick look for casualties, then I'll knock the fire down'.*

Now, old Trevor knew the products of the fire, and any steam created putting it out were going to travel up the stairwell (along the outlet flowpath) as there were no other ventilation points to exhaust gases to (basement lights etc.), so he told me to get away from the door. Everything was going to plan. Until...

A second crew were committed, who in their best 'Cowboy' style came flying down the stairs at a rate of knots, opening the nozzle fully and direct cooling the fuel bed. In the process getting tangled up with Trevor and myself, limbs tangled everywhere all at the bottom of the stairs.

Now this would have been comical and, to be fair to the second crew, they did put the fire out, however their attack created a great deal of steam and it could only exit along that flowpath, now blocked by four tangled firefighters. We were lucky that Nomex bunker gear was around by this time and we got away with some lobster-red skin, looking like British tourists on a Mediterranean vacation. Had it been the previous PPE incarnation of woollen tunics, plastic 'wetlegs' and gardener's gloves, we could all have been scalded severely, if not killed.

Our friend and fire service sage Professor Stefan Svensson of Lund University, states that 'steam is not a problem', and he is right. Steam production is not a problem provided that the flowpath that the steam will follow is known and controlled and that, unlike myself & Trevor, firefighters do not place themselves between the fire and the exhaust on the outlet flowpath.

However, for a firefighter who is 'external'/defensive, directing water onto the fuel bed from a position outside such as through a window, from a turntable ladder cage/ 'bucket', then this is the way to go. (Provided, of course, that we have nobody inside.)

If the firefighter is inside then they need to make a professional decision on what effect direct cooling will have on conditions, noting the inlet/outlet flowpaths, the 3D environment, the presence of gaseous fuels and what the likely outcome of direct cooling will be. Too much steam in a small compartment can also cause increased heat due to a phenomenon called 'thermal inversion'. We will cover this later in the chapter.

Without confusing things too much, there are a number of methods of direct cooling.

Let's think about it. If we fully open the nozzle and direct a forceful jet into a fuel bed the pressure will agitate it, possibly driving burning materials up into the gaseous fuels which, if they are within flammable range, will ignite and cause problems.

Despite popular opinion, firefighters can be gentle and have a light touch. A commonplace method of direct cooling is known as 'painting' whereby a gentle flow of water from the nozzle is gently applied in a 'brush stroke' fashion to cool the burning materials without disrupting them.

'Pencilling' is another technique where water is 'lobbed' onto burning materials by projecting a short burst that is dropped from above directly onto the burning materials. Again, the point of this is to not disrupt, destroy or agitate the burning materials too much.

Indirect cooling

Indirect cooling, as the name suggests, takes place where direct cooling is not possible.

Water is deflected from walls and ceilings etc. onto burning materials. By doing this, compartment boundaries are also cooled which can slow the radiation of heat back into the fire compartment from those surfaces and prevent or slow pyrolysis of any surfaces not yet fully involved in the fire.

Indirect cooling is a useful technique when entry to a compartment is not crucial and the 'fuel bed' cannot be clearly seen or located. It can be deployed to great effect. A possible negative effect is that it will create huge amounts of steam, but as long as we are not on a flowpath and/or we don't have casualties or firefighters within the compartment then we are able to utilise this.

The steam that is created can be, by controlling flowpath and "sealing" a compartment, acts as a suppression technique and can inert fire gases in the compartment. This can then be followed up with an interior attack.

Gas cooling

Gas cooling is so widely misunderstood and viewed with suspicion that we are going to try and simplify it as much as possible here. Starting with what we know:

- Smoke is the by-product of incomplete combustion and along with a very long list of toxic and carcinogenic particles and gases, it also contains unburnt fuel.
- PVT are related – reduce temperature and we reduce the volume of gases.
- Heat transfers from hot areas to less hot areas, heating them in the process through conduction, convection, radiation.
- Passive materials absorb energy in heat form.
- Fire gases exist in flammable ranges depending on their concentration with air.
- It uses heat energy to create steam from water.

So, having established the basics above, let's look at what happens when we apply water into heated fire gas.

Energy gets transferred from the hot fire gas into the water. This reduces the temperature of the fire gases which in turn reduces the volume (PVT) resulting in less gaseous fuel to ignite.

What about steam though?

Because there is such energy required to vaporise steam, and the original fire gases have now been reduced in volume, the result is that there remains less steam/fire gas mix than the original volume of fire gas. Or, more simply, when we cool the gases, we may create six units of steam, but if we have reduced the volume of fire gases by 10 units, we have a net reduction of gases by 4 units. We shrink the gaseous fuels by PVT principles, reducing temperature, reducing volume.

However, we need to be careful not to create too much steam. And this may happen fairly easily:

- Everybody quotes a 1700:1 expansion ratio at 100°c of water to steam.
- But at 500°c this can be as high as 5000:1.
- Five litres of liquid water can become 25 cubic metres of steam.

This has to go somewhere, along a flowpath, or it will disrupt the buoyancy of gases in a compartment, getting above the fire gases, occupying the space and pushing fire gases downwards onto casualties or Firefighters. The temperature levels within a compartment get 'flipped'. This is known as 'thermal inversion' and is a real risk from over application of water in closed compartments.

How do we ensure that we don't create too much steam?

This is where pulsation or pulsing has its application. To show why though we need to be aware of something called 'water droplet theory' but fear not, for we'll simplify using a vegetable.

Let's think of an onion as a droplet of water. If we have a large onion it has many more layers than a small onion. If we projected our large onion (water) into the heated fire gases, then the first few layers would absorb that heat energy from the fire gas and turn to steam while shrinking the fire gases. However, several layers of the onion would get through, striking the superheated surfaces, and while a layer or two may have a cooling effect there, the remaining layers all get turned to steam.

If we have a tiny onion with fewer layers, the layers may all be turned to steam, absorbing heat from the atmosphere even before they enter the fire gas layer, and can absorb any heat energy and reduce the volume of those fire gases or produce steam.

By process of elimination, we need the right size onion, with enough layers to absorb heat energy in the gas layer, but not so many that excess layers break through the fire gases, striking surfaces and turning to steam.

This is until we can safely apply water onto the fuel bed with knowledge of the flowpath taken by steam generated. Remember, put the fire out and reduce other risks!

Therefore, when cooling gases, we need the right size water droplets. These are applied in the right quantity to absorb the maximum amount of heat, without excess water striking super-heated surfaces and turning to steam.

Cooling the gases reduces their volume, it allows Firefighters to safely progress to a position to fully extinguish the fire. It is a means to that end. A method of making safe progress reducing the potential for rapid fire developments and gases to ignite cutting of our exit and trapping us inside the risk.

> **For firefighters, what does all this mean for me?**
>
> Put quite simply, these are the tools you have to keep yourself and your teammates safe, which reduces the risks to us, allows us to save people that we can save and get the fire out.
>
> It's about having the knowledge to use the correct methods, observe and understand the effect that we are having on the fire and the fire gases, adjust our approach if appropriate, be able to forecast the outcome of what we intend to do and avoid negative outcomes. It's a series of thought processes and questions.
>
> In short, what are we doing? What should we be doing? What will happen when we do it?
>
> Are we safely moving towards a position where we can put this out? If so, which method is best to use? If not, are we endangering ourselves and others by not intervening swiftly enough? Have we addressed the gaseous fuels of the 3D environment? Are we putting enough water on/up or too little? Are we controlling the flowpaths and steam?

Flow rates

Flow rates are perhaps the most misunderstood concept in the UK and European fire rescue services. There seems to be more appreciation of this concept in North America, but let's revisit the basics, using the principles that we have worked through together in the previous chapters of this book.

Paul Grimwood wrote about the dangers of not having enough flow in September 2000's *FIRE* magazine. To paraphrase:

'Due to the small containers (flashover chambers) that we have traditionally practised gas cooling in the UK in, there has been a misinterpretation that a high pressure hose reel

jet offering less than 110 litres per minute (lpm) is sufficient for compartment firefighting as it will not create too much steam, very difficult to cause thermal inversion and so on.'

This is wrong.

Let's also consider that in these training facilities we only use stranded board or possibly light timber as fuel. We haven't got a room full of 'high energy materials' that are full of energy and burning potential.

If we remember heat release rates from an earlier chapter, we can compare them to the practical cooling capabilities of water at certain flow rates.

Tables from *FIRE* magazine September, 2000, Grimwood:

Practical cooling capabilities of water	
LPM	ENERGY ABSORPTION
50	0.7MW
100	1.4MW
150	2.1MW
200	2.8MW
300	4.2MW
550	7.7MW
800	11.2 MW
1000	14 MW

Let us compare this with the heat release rate of common furniture:

ITEM	HEAT RELEASE RATE
Sofa (2 seat)	3.0MW
Sofa (3 seat)	3.5MW
Upholstered Chair	2.0MW
Small trashcan	0.3MW
Single Mattress	1.0MW
Pine Bunk-beds	4.5MW
3 side workstation	7.0MW

So, if we combine these two tables let's take a look at what we would require in terms of flow:

ITEM	HEAT RELEASE RATE MW	FLOW RATE LPM
Sofa (2 seat)	3.0MW	300
Sofa (3 seat)	3.5MW	300
Upholstered Chair	2.0MW	150
Small trashcan	0.3MW	50
Single Mattress	1.0MW	100
Pine Bunk-beds	4.5MW	550
3 side workstation	7.0MW	550

As we know, however, fires do not involve one particular item in isolation like this. There is every possibility that a living room will involve, for example, at least one chair and a sofa, plus a small table, a television set and other materials. Realistically, a living room fire may well have a combined heat release rate in excess of 9 MW.

If we refer back to the cooling capabilities table, we can see that we are looking at 800 litres per minute flow requirement to successfully cool involved materials for one living room/lounge stocked up with 'high energy materials.

The maximum HRR generated in a flashover chamber/CFBT container is 1.5MW, and while these are a great tool for demonstration and practice, the firefighter and incident commander needs to remain mindful that they do not reflect true conditions on the incident ground.

In two line of duty death (LODD) incidents in the UK, firefighters attempted to tackle blazes containing sufficient loading to generate high heat release rates, with high pressure hose reel jets delivering, at most, only 120LPM. This low flow rate was never going to extinguish those fires or cool those materials, and as we repeat, 'extinguish the fire and reduce other risks.

We have used article from 15 years ago to illustrate this – flow rate is of the utmost importance. The two LODD incidents I refer to occurred in the UK in 2004 and 2007. Sadly, it didn't appear that the knowledge and information about flow rates was picked up or disseminated to firefighters at the time or even in the intervening years. You are making the choice by reading this book, to be informed and to honour those who died by not making the same mistakes.

Chapter 10: revision questions

- List three methods of water application.

- Excessive steam creation is not a problem if what is controlled?

- Describe what happens when we apply water into fire gases.

- What is the effect of using water droplets that are too small?

- List two dangers of using insufficient flow rates.

- If flowpaths are not controlled, which phenomena can occur if excessive steam is created by firefighters applying water?

- Give two examples of when we may use indirect cooling.

- Exercise – estimate the combined HRR of items in your living room.

International Compartment Fire Behaviour Training Instructor Course:

This chapter covers the information needed for the following learning outcomes;

Learning Outcome	Description
3	Understand the tactics, tools and techniques used by firefighters to deal with and prevent fire development within a compartment
3.1	Explain offensive/internal attack, transitional attack, and defensive/external attack strategies
3.2	Identify nozzle techniques that may be suited to internal attack, transitional attack and external attack
3.3	Explain ventilations tactics and techniques that can be synergistically combined with various nozzle techniques
3.4	Explain compartment entry procedures/techniques and the concept of the kill zone, buffer zone and safe zone

5.5	Explain how ventilation tactics/techniques can be combined with suppression tactic/techniques to increase the overall safety and efficiency
6	Demonstrate firefighting techniques prior to, and after entry to the compartment kill zone
6.1	Apply methods of gaining entry into a compartment that mitigate adverse conditions for entrapped occupants and firefighters
6.2	Analyse the potential benefit of applying transitional attack prior to internal attack
6.3	Analyse the possibility of utilising/making exhaust openings near the fire prior to entry
6.4	Make entry into a kill zone after using techniques that allow for a SAHF assessment of interior conditions, cooling of the internal environment, displacement of loose overhead hazards, sweeping away of hazards at floor level
6.5	Buffer the route through the kill zone by using techniques that confine the fire/smoke, cool the gases and linings
6.6	Apply ventilation techniques that may compliment the chosen extinguishing techniques

The following videos assist with understanding of this chapter- find them at the YouTube channel: **Ben Walker & Shan Raffel Firefighter Training;**
tinyurl.com/2xaeb4yu

Video and Hyperlinks:
The Theory Behind "Gas-Cooling" https://tinyurl.com/49wejkr2
"Gas Cooling" effects before making a direct fire attack seen in thermal image https://tinyurl.com/mss56x74
"Gas Cooling" versus "Cooling Gases" https://tinyurl.com/teu5fju8
Effect of closing doors/ "anti-ventilation" https://tinyurl.com/4ex5cs6m
Nozzle and Door Entry Techniques https://tinyurl.com/2pp6fvxa
Gas Cooling in a live fire training burn https://tinyurl.com/5ehsxuce
Gas Cooling followed by direct attack https://tinyurl.com/fd6pf8h8

Chapter 11: Fire dynamics – 'notable events'

This chapter takes a simplistic look at fire dynamics behaviours at a number of high-profile incidents that occurred within the UK, which sadly resulted in line of duty deaths.

The aspects of fire dynamics that we look at here are not in any way a complete list of factors involved in those incidents, but we shall be evaluating a portion of them without judgement or prejudice in order to relate what occurred to our knowledge of fire dynamics gathered so far in this book. Naturally, there were far more factors and subtleties to these incidents and the fire dynamics that occurred. This is merely an initial pointer, with some basic abstracts. I would encourage anyone reading this to study these incidents in far more depth and challenge yourself to develop a deeper understanding of them.

We are not looking to criticise decisions made, either at a task or operational level, of which we have the benefit of hindsight, analysis and, sadly, loss.

This chapter is dedicated to those firefighters who lost their lives in the discharge of their duties at the following incidents:

- Blaina, South Wales, 1996
- Harrow Court, Stevenage, 2004
- Bethnal Green Road, London, 2004
- Shirley Towers, Hampshire, 2009

The Institution of Fire Engineers has an extensive database of Firefighter Safety incidents that have been contributed to by many but has been extensively and commendably worked on by Adam Course of Avon Fire & Rescue Service for many years. It is available at this link;

https://www.ife.org.uk/Firefighter-Safety

Fire behaviour case study 1: Zephania Way, Blaina, South Wales

In memory of FF Griffin and FF Lane.

This incident occurred in the South Wales village of Blaina in 1996. 'Retained' (volunteer/paid on call) crews were called to reports of a fire on the ground floor of a two level, terraced house with two children unaccounted for. In fact, there had actually only been one child missing, who was rescued following the initial entry by the firefighters.

Due to delays gaining access to the property (parked vehicles obstructing the fire appliance), the fire had been burning for some time before the arrival of the first crew.

The figure below shows a cross-sectional diagram of the property:

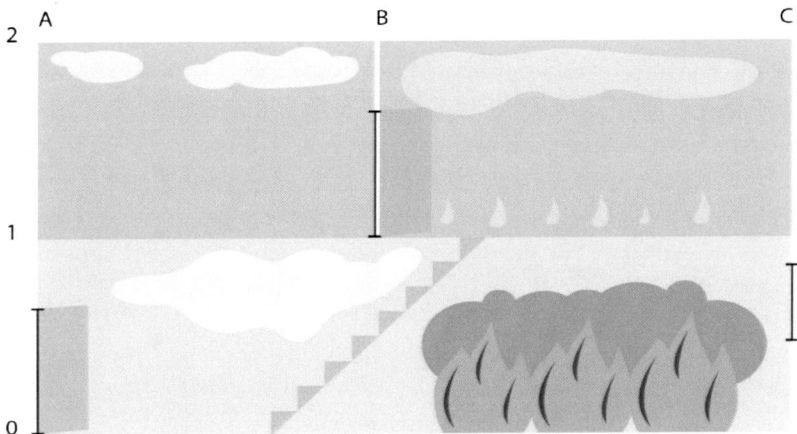

Key:
Floor 1, B-C: Heat from kitchen fire causes pyrolysis at floor level (above fire) - Flammable products releases and mixes with air.
Firefighters make first entry and perform a "snatch rescue" - in the process doors A0 and B1 are opened - this allows the pyrolysis products to spread into further compartments and dilute into flammable range.

The fire is being shown at the rear (right) of the property. As the volume and temperature increased, so did the pressure of the gases (PVT).

The possible effects of this include:

Heat from the fire compartment heated the ceiling and underside of the first floor. This caused the floor element and low level contents such as carpets and possibly furniture to pyrolyse and release gaseous fuels into the room upstairs, which when mixed with the available air, diluted or concentrated into their flammable range.

Another suggestion is that, due to poor workmanship, gases under pressure were able to travel through gaps around ducting or next to pipework and accumulate in the room above the fire compartment, again, within their flammable range.

As we know, from our rapid fire development chapters, these are the ingredients of a fire gas ignition, minus the ignition source.

The firefighters re-entered via the front door (left of picture) and proceeded upstairs to continue a search for the reported missing child. This created a flowpath where higher pressure fire gases could exit to lower pressures outside.

While entering the upstairs room in an atmosphere of fire gases within their flammable range, an ignition source was provided. It has been argued that fire breached the floor, providing flame as an ignition source, or perhaps that the fire compartment window failed along with the upstairs window above it, allowing egress and ingress of flame to act as an ignition source.

The ignition was accompanied by a supersonic-pressure wave (detonation), which travelled along the path of least resistance (the flowpath created), causing fatal blast injuries to the fire crew.

The subsequent negative pressure phase caused the entry point door to 'suck' shut, crimping a 19mm high pressure hose reel tubing and hampering any rescue attempts made by emergency crews thereafter.

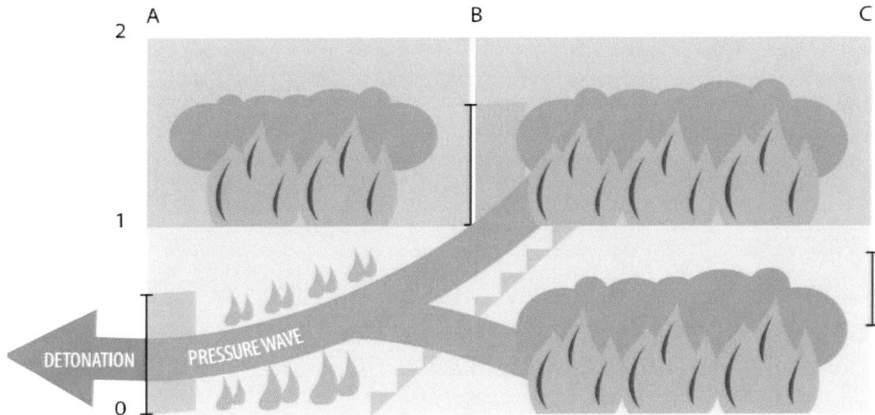

Firefighters make second entry at which point fire breaks through (ducting or window/floor failure) igniting accumulated flammable gases in room above kitchen - as these products have spread throughout the property all gases ignite. As per P.V.T principle higher pressure moves to lower pressure. As this was accompanied with a supersonic pressure wave it was classed as "detonation". The subsequent negative reaction pressure wave closed door A0 crimping hose line.

For firefighters, to revise our prior knowledge, let's consider the following

We know that smoke is unburnt gaseous fuel.
Smoke in rooms or compartments that we know to be remote from the fire compartment is a classic indicator of potential fire gas ignition conditions. Crews should be vigilant and aware of this, and prepare to withdraw or take necessary actions to deal with these circumstances.
Remember:
Extinguish the fire as a priority as this significantly reduces all other risks.

Fire gases will move to areas of lower pressure (PVT).

We must consider the effects of opening and closing doors, creating flowpaths, and understand how this will cause fire gases to move and fire to develop (PVT).

Cooling gases will reduce their temperature and volume (PVT) and if steam is created this will reduce the potential for these gases to ignite.

Blaina was one of the first incidents in the UK to be categorised as a fire gas explosion/fire gas ignition. Its devastating consequences have amplified the absolute necessity for firefighters to understand the '3D' nature of the environment that we operate in, and the risks that fire dynamics present. Honour their sacrifice by ensuring that the whole of your team, your crew or your watch know the signs and symptoms.

The following videos assist with understanding of this chapter- find them at the YouTube channel: **Ben Walker & Shan Raffel Firefighter Training; tinyurl.com/2xaeb4yu**

Video and Hyperlinks:
Sky News- 1st February 1996 https://tinyurl.com/yte2f5k8
IFE Interest of Special Interest https://tinyurl.com/y4dveh29

Fire behaviour case study 2: Harrow Court, Stevenage, 2004

In memory of FF Wornham and FF Miller.

Harrow Court is a typical UK residential high-rise dwelling, containing a number of apartments. On the day in question, firefighters were called to a reported fire upon the 14th floor of this building.

Upon arrival, crews reported the presence of smoke exiting from a window on the upper floor. When they reached the compartment, the Leading Firefighter (Lt) reported that wispy grey smoke was issuing from the gaps at the top of the door.

For firefighters, revising what we have learnt

If we can see smoke exiting in this manner, we could look for the 'splayed' pattern or 'pulsing/ belching' that suggests that a window is on the upwind side and we potentially have wind driving into the fire compartment and further pressurising the gases inside, creating turbulent gas flows, increasing the speed of fire development and suggesting that at the moment there may only be double flowpath (both in and out or 'bidirectional flowpath').

Therefore, as we have seen, we should be extremely cautious not to create a 'unidirectional' flowpath, especially with ourselves inside it, like a tube.

The smoke that the officer observed from the gaps at the top of the door suggest that there was a pressurised situation inside. This could be an indicator of not only a wind driven fire, but also of potential backdraught.

Due to the UK legislation, buildings over 18 metres yet smaller than 60 metres are required to have a 'dry' rising main (standpipe). This has to be charged and pressurised from an outlet on a floor below. It's good practice to have two lines fully charged with the ability to advance a 'covering hoseline' beyond an 'attack line' in case of emergencies or a 'covered retreat' has to be instigated. More of this shall be covered in Volume 3 "Fighting Fire".

Due to a delay in getting adequate equipment and hoselines charged and in position, the crew committed without any firefighting media in order to attempt a 'snatch' rescue of an occupant.

At this time, wind was entering the apartment on the North West side of the building, wind speeds recorded at approximately 23mph at the height of 50m (14th floor).

It is thought that the firefighters created a flow path when making entry, or that the failure of the windows of the north east side of the building created a unidirectional flowpath, with pressurised and turbulent gas flows facilitating extremely rapid fire development.

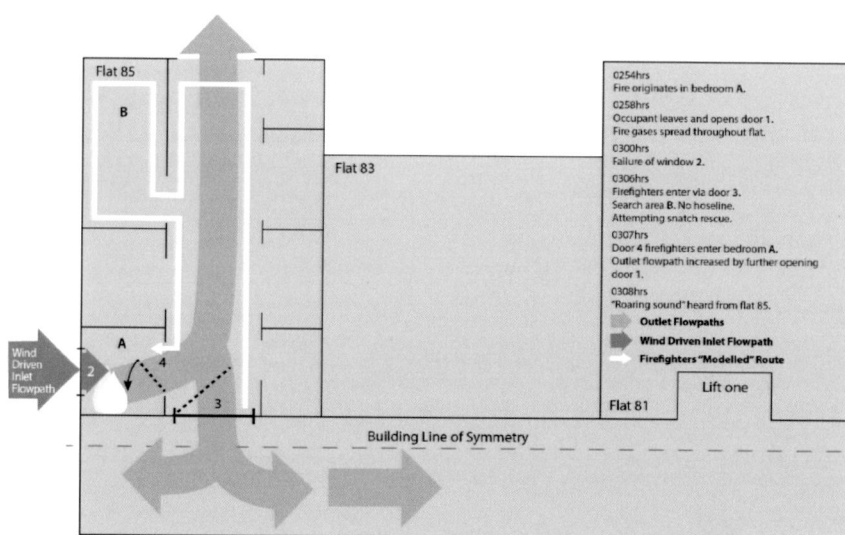

Grimwood, FBU Report

This fire was later estimated through fire modelling to be burning at 8.5-10MW post flashover.

For firefighters, to revise our prior knowledge let us consider the following

When attending high rises, we need to be aware of what are the conditions and wind direction is telling us.

In this case, as the wind was moving in a west-north-westerly direction (coming from the north west). In situations such as this, we have to be conscious that if we approach from downwind, which may be the only approach available, we have every possibility of creating a unidirectional flowpath or fire 'fatal funnel'. We are, in effect, in the 'KILL ZONE'.

We know that the pressure of wind can cause turbulent gas flows and allow fire to develop more quickly and spread faster. This intensity and heat release will demand certain flow rates to enable the fuels to be extinguished and the fire to be bought under control.

This pressurisation caused by the wind can present itself as signs and symptoms of other rapid fire developments too, such as the pulsation or belching from windows on the upwind side, fire gases being forced out of gaps under pressure on the downwind side.

We should therefore be aware and prepared for this type of situation, with knowledge of flowpath management, sufficient flowrate in our hoselines, charged and ready to go, and proceed with caution.

The following information assists with understanding of this chapter- additional videos are at our YouTube channel: **Ben Walker & Shan Raffel Firefighter Training;** tinyurl.com/2xaeb4yu

Hyperlinks:
Mark Fishlock Presentation on Harrow Court https://tinyurl.com/dtb9hnt3
IFE Incident of Special Interest https://tinyurl.com/j96y9444

Fire behaviour case study 3: Bethnal Green Road, London, 2004

In memory of FF Faust and FF Meere

Crews were called out to reports of smoke issuing from a textiles/clothing shop on Bethnal Green Road. A cross section of the building is provided in the figure below.

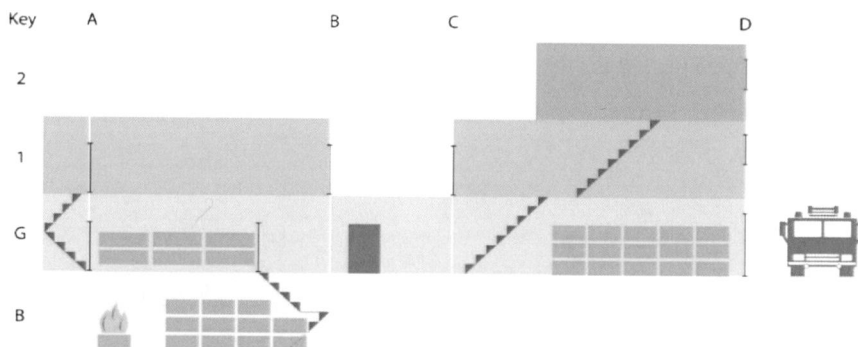

The fire crew's arrival point was the front of the building, denoted by the fire truck.

The fire had started in the basement at the rear of the building (seen at the bottom left of the figure). The basement was extremely congested with fabrics, clothing, material and boxes. These had been stacked upon milk crates which created a gap of approximately 18 inches between the floor and the underside of the available fuels. In a 'convection cycle', this allowed a continual supply of cool air to be drawn towards the fire without impediment.

Due to being unable to gain access from the ground floor, crews had initially made entry via a first floor window to the building (D1), where it became apparent that the heat was rising from the ground floor. The forced breaking of a window here to gain entry created a bi-directional flowpath.

Crews were subsequently able to gain entry via the ground floor following the removal of a security roller shutter (DG), creating another flowpath which they were unable to shut. They were also able to gain entry from a side alley (denoted here between points B and C on floor G).

For firefighters, what should you be aware of?

While there is a significant amount of fuel, due to the location of the fire in the basement there may not be sufficient oxygen to sustain burning, resulting in a ventilation controlled situation. However, due to the milk crates enhancing an inlet flowpath towards the fire, it also has the potential to develop quickly if air is transmitted to it along this flowpath.

Crews have forced entry to the first floor, twice on the ground floor, and crews have also now opened doors between the front and rear superstructures of the building.

If we look to the rear (far left) there is also a stairwell from the ground to the first floor. Once crews opened the doors at the position denoted 'venting crew' we have a situation with five inlets and outlets for the ingress of air to feed the fire, and for buoyant, heated, pressurised fire gases to escape to areas of lower pressures.

With a number of gas flows colliding within the building, this causes turbulence, which as we know causes faster fire development and increased burning velocity and flame speeds. If sufficient pressure exists, we also know that they can detonate and move faster than the speed of sound.

In this case, the development of the fire was influenced by the flowpaths created by crews. The heat from the fire also caused materials above it, on the ground floor, to pyrolyse, and once these gases within were flammable range, to ignite. Turbulent gas flows, extreme temperatures and pressurised gaseous fuels all contributed to the rapid escalation of this fire. Sadly, the position of the firefighters meant they were positioned in the 'Kill Zone' on an outlet flowpath.

For firefighters, what can we learn from Bethnal Green?

It is vital to remember the importance of understanding and controlling flowpaths, gas flows and being aware of the signs and symptoms of impending rapid fire developments, alongside flow-rates and water application.

Sadly, Bethnal Green gives us pause for thought for a number of reasons.

Flow rate and water application is of primary importance – we need sufficient water to put the fire out when we get to a position to do so. Learn the flow rates and likely fire loading that they can deal with, so we don't go in underprepared. Let's not take a knife to a tank battle!

Creating flowpaths can work to our advantage but also to our disadvantage. It is unlikely that we can use multiple flowpaths to our advantage due to the turbulence caused by the gas flows mixing and colliding.

Pyrolysis is the chemical decomposition of a substance by heat. Once crews witnessed pyrolysis on the floor above the basement ("white smoke is fuel"), they should have been aware of the extreme heat they were dealing with. If we remember PVT, that kind of temperature will be producing large quantities of fire gas (gaseous fuels) and probably a lot of pressure. When these co-exist, it is an indicator that rapid development may be imminent.

The following information assists with understanding of this chapter- additional videos are at our YouTube channel: Ben Walker & Shan Raffel Firefighter Training; tinyurl.com/2xaeb4yu

Hyperlinks:
East London Advertiser- Memorial laid to Firefighters killed in line of duty https://tinyurl.com/mcdpmh8c
British Broadcasting Corporation- on firemens deaths https://tinyurl.com/mrn3fuvf

Fire Behaviour Case Study 4: Shirley Towers, Portsmouth

In memory of FF Shears and FF Bannon.

Crews were mobilised to respond to a high-rise domestic dwelling fire on the 9th floor of a building containing approximately 150 apartments, distributed over multiple levels as per the following 2 figures.

A carelessly placed curtain (drape) on top of a lamp caused an ignition in the lounge, which the occupant was unable to extinguish with a soft-drink bottle. The occupant then left the apartment, and the fire service was summoned.

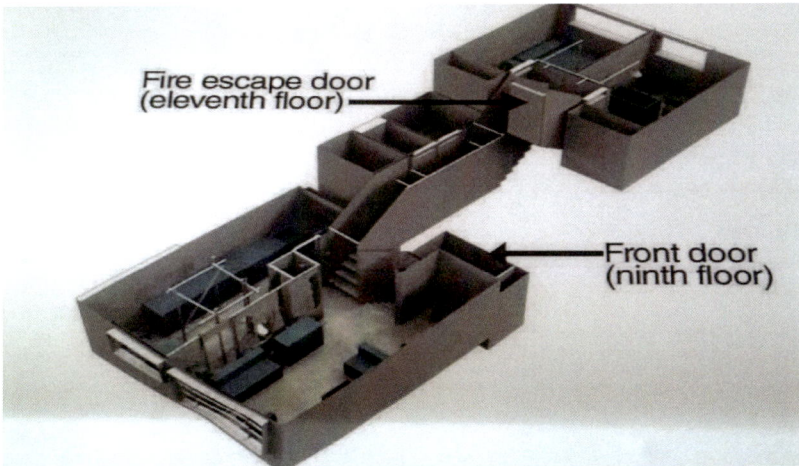

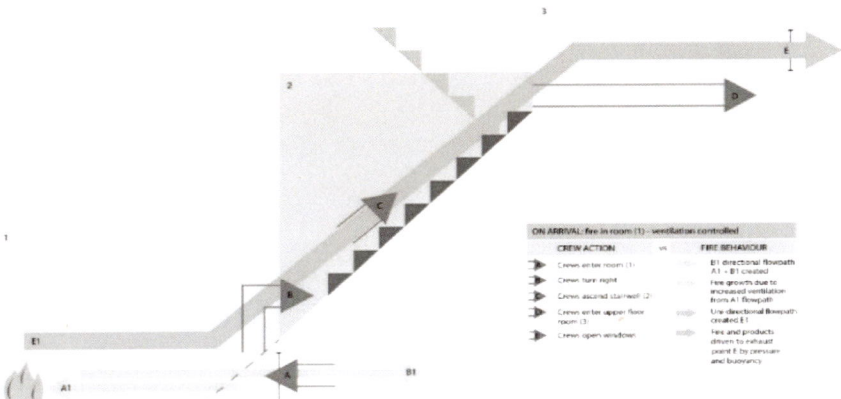

You can see in the second figure that the fire was located in the lounge area. Due to the designated 'search route' the two crews proceeded up the internal stairs, bypassing the fire compartment, unable to locate the fire due to intense smoke (suggesting a low neutral plane – an indicator of a ventilation controlled situation and that we should beware of creating flowpaths). In effect they turned their backs on the fire and proceeded upwards.

Reaching the two bedrooms (top right of the first figure) the firefighters opened the windows for ventilation, thereby creating a distinct outlet flowpath. This created an ingress of air through the entry door to feed the fire and assist combustion, and two outlets or 'exhausts' at a higher level. The natural buoyancy and the pressure of the gas caused it to move towards the windows the crews had opened, in effect creating a 'chimney effect'. The firefighters were also positioned between the fire and the exhaust vent, in the 'fatal funnel' or 'Kill Zone'.

While two firefighters managed to escape via an exit door to the 11th floor, two firefighters didn't.

For firefighters, what can we learn about fire dynamics from this?

Like Blaina, Bethnal Green and Harrow Court, there are a number of lessons and learning points across all areas of the fire service response. However, with regard to fire dynamics, Shirley Towers is perhaps the clearest example of two of the points that we have repeated many times throughout this book.

1. Locate and extinguish the fire and reduce the other risks. This was the original brief of the crew, however, tragically they passed the fire. This highlights the importance of frequent compartment fire training and the use of equipment such as thermal imaging cameras.

2. Recognise, understand and control flowpaths. Throughout the course of this book, we have emphasised the critical nature of this – knowing that PVT means that when we create a flowpath, pressurised, heated gases will move towards areas of lower pressure and we do not want to be caught between the source and the outlet! Furthermore, by providing a source of air (oxygen) to the fire, we can increase its rate of development, change its ventilation profile and reduce our time frame for making a successful intervention to extinguish it.

The following videos assist with understanding of this chapter- find them at the YouTube channel: **Ben Walker & Shan Raffel Firefighter Training;** tinyurl.com/2xaeb4yu

Video and Hyperlinks:
On Demand News- Southampton Firefighters Killed
https://tinyurl.com/ysft8wwc
IFE- Incident of Special Interest
https://tinyurl.com/4e899824

Chapter summary

These line of duty deaths have certain factors that are relevant to each. The effect of airflow and flowpath featured in each of these incidents. Let's close this chapter by recalling the words of James Braidwood from his 1866 book *Fire Prevention and Fire Extinction.*

'On the first discovery of a fire, it is of the utmost consequence to shut, and keep shut, all doors, windows, or other openings. It may often be observed, after a house has been on fire, that one floor is comparatively untouched, while those above and below are nearly burned out. This arises from the door on that particular floor having been shut, and the draught directed elsewhere. If the person who has examined the fire finds a risk of its gaining ground upon him, he should, if within reach of fire-engines, keep everything close, and await their arrival, instead of admitting air to the fire by ineffectual efforts to oppose it with inadequate means.'

(Braidwood, p63, London, 1866)

Braidwood knew the danger of creating flowpaths that admitted air to the fire and the creation of 'draughts' (flowpaths) in 1866. It's imperative that we act as custodians of that knowledge and understand and implement it effectively within the course of our duties.

JAMES BRAIDWOOD.

The fact that the advice we give to the general public is to shut doors when exiting a property on fire to confine it to one area, restricting its development and causing a 'ventilation controlled' situation, is wasted if we approach fires without careful consideration for these factors. Often tragic consequences.

'*The more things change … the more they stay the same.*'
Braidwood's words are as relevant today as they were 150 years ago.
This has been the motivation for the creation of this manual. A
practical guide to help the Firefighters on the ground.

Chapter 12: Conclusion

As we approach the end of this basic introduction to fire dynamics, I hope that we have introduced some basics, clarified some points and fuelled our knowledge to learn more about this interesting and risk critical area.

Hopefully you will move onto more in-depth and technical publications to build upon the foundations that you may have received from this book.

Of course, I hope you join us for the volume 2 of the books; "Reading Fire"- A complete guide to scene assessment and volume 3 "Fighting Fire"- tactics and techniques.

Most importantly, we really want to hear your thoughts. If you think that this book has been helpful or not, please feel free to contact us through www.benwalkerfirefighter.com and shan.raffel@gmail.com and share your opinions. Remember, this book is merely an introduction and a start to your own journey out there in the fire service.

Keep learning, seek excellence, take care, and make firefighter safety your priority.

"Fighting Fires with Squad One of the Chicago Fire Department".

CFBT Instructor Level 1 and 2 at Falck, Rotterdam 2018

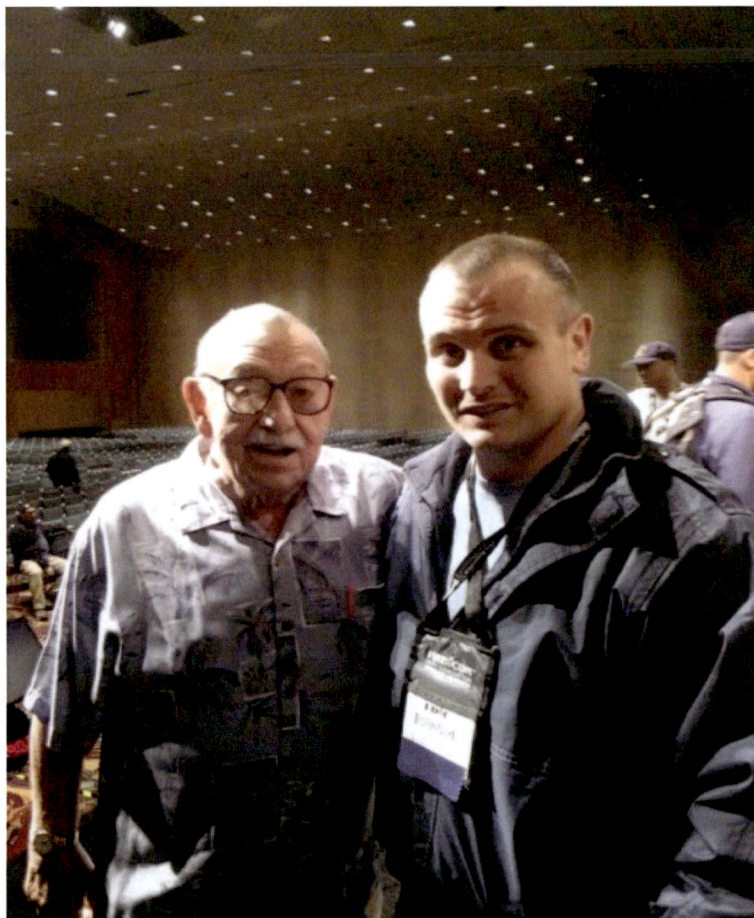

Feeling the force with legendary Chief and Incident Command Guru Alan Brunacini

References:

Books:

Braidwood, J (1866). *Fire Prevention & Fire Extinction.* (1st ed.). London: Bell & Daldy.

Brunacini, N. (2012). Staring into the Sun. (1st ed.) Phoenix: Nick Brunacini Publications

John D. DeHaan, 2002. *Kirk's Fire Investigation (5th Edition).* 5 Edition. Prentice Hall.

Drysdale, D (2011). *An Introduction to Fire Dynamics.* 3rd ed. Edinburgh: Willey

Gregory E. Gorbett, James, L. Pharr,2010. *Fire Dynamics.* 1st Edition. Prentice Hall.

Grimwood, P (2008). *Euro Firefighter.* Huddersfield, England: Jeremy Mills Publishing.

Grimwood, P et al (2005). *3D Firefighting.* (1st ed.). United States: University of Oregon press.

Institution of Fire Engineers (2004). *Elementary Fire Engineering Handbook.*(3rd Edition) Leicester. IFE publications

Manuals:

Crown Copyright (1997). *Fire Service Manual Volume 2: Compartment Fires & Tactical Ventilation.* London. The Stationary Office.

Crown Copyright (1998). *Fire Service Manual Volume 1: Physics & Chemistry for Firefighters.* London. The Stationary Office

Crown Copyright. (2001) *Fire Service Manual Volume 3: Basic Principles of Building & Construction.* London. The Stationary Office

"Diethyl Ether - Safety Properties". Wolfram|Alpha.
Fuels and Chemicals - Autoignition Temperatures, engineeringtoolbox.com
Cafe, Tony. *"PHYSICAL CONSTANTS FOR INVESTIGATORS".* tcforensic.com.au. TC Forensic P/L.

Retrieved 11 February 2015.
"Butane - Safety Properties". Wolfram|Alpha.
Tony Cafe. "Physical Constants for Investigators". Journal of Australian Fire Investigators.
(Reproduced from "Firepoint" magazine)
"Flammability and flame retardancy of leather". leathermag.com. Leather International /
Global Trade Media. Retrieved 11 February 2015.
"Hydrogen - Safety Properties". Wolfram|Alpha.
Forest Products Laboratory (1964). "Ignition and charring temperatures of wood" (PDF). Forest
Service U. S. Department of Agriculture.

Websites:

Fishlock, M. 2012. *High Rise Firefighting co uk*. [Online]. [July 2015]. Available from: http://www.highrisefirefighting.co.uk

Hartin, E. 2010. *Compartment Fire Behaviour Training-United States*. [Online]. [July 2015]. Available from: http://www.cfbt-us.com

United States Department of Commerce: National Institute of Standards & Technology [Online] [July 2015] http://www.nist.gov/fire/

NASA- Research Materials- original no longer available

Unknown Author: www.greenmaltese.com

Raffel, S. Understanding the Language of Fire: Be Safe https://www.fireengineering.com/leadership/shan-raffel-understanding-the-language-of-fire-be-safe-think-be-sahf/.

Journals:

Grimwood, P. 2000. Compartment Firefighting: Finding the right flow rates. *FIRE magazine*. 1(September), Pavilion Publications.

Burgess, MJ & Wheeler, RV. 1911 The lower limit of inflammation of mixtures of the paraffin hydrocarbons with air. Journal of the Chemical Society

Thesis:

Dave, J. 2012"Heat Release Rate- the single most important variable in fire". MSc Fire Dynamics dissertation, University of Leeds, United Kingdom.

Additional Documentation:

"Course Materials":
Level 1 Fire Investigators Course "Fire Dynamics" courtesy of Tyne & Wear Fire & Rescue Service

Skills for Justice Awards: Level 3 Certificate in the Instruction of Compartment Fire Behaviour Training.

Tyne & Wear Fire & Rescue Service: Breathing Apparatus Instructors' Course materials circa 2008 edition

Institution of Fire Engineers- International Compartment Fire Behaviour Instructors' Certification Levels 1,2, Internal Assessor and Verifier qualifications

Reports/Case Studies/Associated Materials:

Institution of Fire Engineers- Firefighter Safety Database- Adam Course

Harrow Court Report: Fire Brigades' Union/Paul Grimwood

Shirley Towers Report: Hampshire FRS, Hampshire Constabulary, Fishlock, M

Bethnal Green Road Report: courtesy of London Fire Brigade personnel.

Blaina Report: courtesy of UK Fire & Rescue Service public domain materials citation of report & inquest carried out 1996.

Verbal Information (conferences)/Informal Instruction:

Svensson, Professor Stefan. International Fire Instructors Workshop, Indianapolis 2015.

Agerstrand, Lars. International Fire Instructors Workshop, Indianapolis 2015.

Hartin, Ed. International Fire Instructors Workshop, Indianapolis 2015.

Gough, Dr Bill. Ongoing advice, instruction & guidance 2013 onwards.

Raffel, Shan. Ongoing advice, instruction & guidance 2013 onwards.

Shan.raffel@gmail.com

https://www.aus-rescue.com/

www.CFBT-international.com

https://www.linkedin.com/in/shanraffel/

Wikipedia- Shan Raffel-
https://en.wikipedia.org/wiki/Shan_Raffel

igfirerescue@gmail.com

www.fireandsafetyconsultant.com

Wikipedia- Ben Walker-
https://en.wikipedia.org/wiki/Benjamin_Walker_(firefighter)

Free online training benwalkerfirefighter.moodlecloud.com (limited to 50 participants at once.)

- International Training Instructor Courses, Seminars, Conferences and Online Training

- Live Fire Facility Design, Development, Commission and Installation plus Instructor/Operator Training

- Occupational Health, Safety & Risk Management Services

- Training and Command Courses

- Fire Safety Assessor Courses

- And many more available.

De-Wipe®
After Fire
Hair & Body Wash

- Wash away the risk of cross contamination
- Suitable for all hair and skin types
- Scientifically proven to eliminate toxins in smoke
- Removes stubborn smoke smell after only one wash

www.ingramcontent.com/pod-product-compliance
Lightning Source LLC
Chambersburg PA
CBRC101140030426
42334CB00008B/120